C000311724

SECURING A REW

A selection of other How To Books

Achieving Personal Well-being
Arranging Insurance
Becoming a Father
Building Self-Esteem
Buying a House
Buying a Personal Computer
Caring for Someone at Home
Choosing a Nursing Home
Choosing a Package Holiday
Controlling Anxiety
Coping with Self Assessment
Dealing with a Death in the Family
Dealing with Your Bank
Having a Baby
Helping Your Child To Read
How to Claim State Benefits
How to Plan a Wedding
How to Run a Local Campaign
How to Run a Voluntary Group
How to Start a Business from
   Home
How to Work from Home
Investing in Stocks & Shares

Learning to Counsel
Lose Weight & Keep Fit
Making a Complaint
Making a Video
Making a Wedding Speech
Making Money from Letting
Managing Your Personal
   Finances
Maximising Your Memory
Raising the Successful Child
Saving and Investing
Self-Counselling
Selling Your House
Successful Grandparenting
Successful Single Parenting
Surviving Redundancy
Surviving Your Partner
Taking in Students
Taking Your Driving Tests
Teaching Someone to Drive
Thriving on Stress
Unlocking Your Potential
Working with Children

Other titles in preparation

The How To Series now contains more than 200 titles in the
following categories:

Business & Management
Computer Basics
General Reference
Jobs & Careers
Living & Working Abroad

Personal Finance
Self-Development
Small Business
Student Handbooks
Successful Writing

Please send for a free copy of the latest catalogue for full details
(see back cover for address).

PERSONAL FINANCE

SECURING A REWARDING RETIREMENT

How to really understand pensions and
prepare successfully for your retirement

Norman Toulson

How To Books

Cartoons by Mike Flanagan

British Library Cataloguing in Publication Data
A catalogue record for this book is available from the British Library.

First published in 1998 by How To Books Ltd, 3 Newtec Place,
Magdalen Road, Oxford OX4 1RE, United Kingdom.
Tel: (01865) 793806. Fax: (01865) 248780.

Note: The material contained in this book is set out in good faith for
general guidance and no liability can be accepted for loss or expense
incurred as a result of relying in particular circumstances on statements
made in the book. The law and regulations may be complex and liable to
change, and readers should check the current position with the relevant
authorities before making personal arrangements.

Produced for How To Books by Deer Park Productions.
Typeset by Anneset, Weston-super-Mare, North Somerset.
Printed and bound by Cromwell Press, Trowbridge, Wiltshire.

Contents

List of Illustrations

Preface

What *is* a rewarding retirement? Opinions will differ, but surely everybody will agree that there are two basic needs – somewhere to live and an income on which to live.

A truly rewarding retirement requires more than those features. The chapters that follow offer information and suggestions that it is hoped may help you to achieve security, and more, by your preparations – whether your retirement is just round the corner or more distant, whether you are self-employed, being made redundant, working part-time, getting married or in a non-pensionable job.

There is a military maxim, that 'time spent in reconnaissance is seldom wasted'. 'Reconnaissance' is another word for 'exploring'. This book can help you to explore the world of retirement, in advance, and to prepare yourself for a truly rewarding retirement. Believe me, it is well worth doing.

Norman Toulson

1
Seeing Where You Stand

Why is retirement like an express train, that you first see at a distance? Because it seems to be moving hardly at all, for a while, then speeds up while your attention is taken up elsewhere, and suddenly hurtles towards you at well over 100 miles an hour.

The sooner you recognise this feature of retirement and take account of your pension prospects and opportunities, the better. You will be able to tune the components of your retirement benefits to harmonise with each other and with your needs, and supplement them where necessary. So what are those components?

QUALIFYING FOR THE STATE PENSION

The state pension is the most common source of income in retirement. Most people eventually receive it. (It is often still referred to as the old age pension, although that label became obsolete 50 years ago.)

To qualify for a state retirement pension, one must have attained the state pension age and made the required contributions. They are related to one's earnings between age 16 and pension age.

Pension age
Before World War II the state pension age for both men and women was 65. Early in the War, the government needed to find replacements, in civilian jobs, for men who were being called up for service in the armed forces. They sought to persuade married women to go into industry. Many of them hesitated.

They had always expected that they would stay at home, looking after their husband and family, from the day after they returned from their honeymoons.

Changing the rules
Faced with this reluctance, Parliament lowered the pension age for women to 60, as an inducement. It worked. Many of them

took clerical or manual jobs.

When the War ended and most of the servicemen returned to civilian jobs, nobody risked disturbing a hornet's nest by suggesting equalising the pension ages for men and women again.

Nowadays non-discrimination legislation disapproves of such a gap between qualifying ages for men and women. Sooner or later, something had to be done about it.

Solving a different problem

To have closed the gap by lowering the men's pension age to 60 would have been prohibitively costly. It would have both shortened by five years the time in which the men would have contributed to the cost and lengthened by five years the time in which they would draw their pensions.

In other words, the total amount they contributed, during their years in employment, would have been reduced by about ten per cent; the total amount they would have drawn during their years as pensioners would have increased by about 20 per cent. (These percentages take no account of the variations in the amounts of contributions and pensions, in line with inflation.)

Clearly any suggestion of reducing the pension age for men to 60 was out of the question. But suddenly to require women to wait five years longer, for what they had been looking forward to, would cause an explosion of dissent and protest of nuclear proportions. Subtlety was at a premium.

Finding a radical solution

The 1995 Pensions Act solved the dilemma. It introduced a sliding scale for removing the discrimination by progressively moving the state pension age for women back to 65. The alteration does not affect women who were born before 6 April 1950. It increases the state pension age progressively for women who were born on or after that date. So before the law changed they were not expecting to start drawing pensions during the next 15 years. And they were not even born until at least ten years after the previous change in the state pension age had been made.

Introducing the change gently

The sliding scale takes ten years to achieve its objective fully. The way in which it operates is complex. A formula spelling out in words how it would achieve the transition would baffle most the people who read it.

To avoid doing this, the Act sets out in a table the dates on which women who were born between 6 April 1950 and 5 April 1955 will be able to claim their state pensions. For those who were born on or after 6 April 1955, state pension age is 65.

Seeing how it works

Figure 1 quotes a selection of the items in the table. From these you can deduce the pension dates for women whose dates of birth are *not* shown. For example, Josephine was born on Christmas Day in 1950. That was in the period from 6 December 1950 to 5 January 1951. Figure 1 shows that women born between those dates will reach state pension age on 6 September 2011.

Taking another example
How about Margaret who was born on 28 July 1953? That was between 6 July and 5 August 1953. Those dates are not shown in

Date of birth	Date of reaching state pension age
6 April 1950–5 May 1950	6 May 2010
6 May 1950–5 Jun 1950	6 July 2010
6 Jun 1950–5 Jul 1950	6 Sep 2010
6 Jul 1950–5 Aug 1950	6 Nov 2010
6 Aug 1950–5 Sep 1950	6 Jan 2011
6 Sep 1950–5 Oct 1950	6 Mar 2011
6 Oct 1950–5 Nov 1950	6 May 2011
6 Nov 1950–5 Dec 1950	6 July 2011
6 Dec 1950–5 Jan 1951	6 Sep 2011
6 Jan 1951–5 Feb 1951	6 Nov 2011
6 Feb 1951–5 Mar 1951	6 Jan 2012
6 Mar 1951–5 Apr 1951	6 Mar 2012
6 Apr 1951–5 May 1851	6 May 2012
6 Apr 1952–5 May 1952	6 May 2014
6 Apr 1953–5 May 1953	6 May 2016
6 Apr 1954–5 May 1954	6 May 2018

And finally

6 Mar 1955–5 Apr 1955	6 Mar 2020

Fig. 1. Some examples of the dates on which women who were born between 6 April 1950 and 5 April 1955 will reach state pension age.

Figure 1, but for the corresponding dates in 1950 in the first column the date in the second column is 6 November 2010. Now look at the last four examples in Figure 1, you will see that whereas the gap between successive entries in the first column is one year the corresponding gap in the second column is two years. So because Margaret was born three years after the birth date we have looked up in Figure 1, we need to add six years to the second column date, *ie* her pension date will be 6 November 2016. To check on the accuracy of this you can note that on that date she will be between her 63rd and 64th birthdays.

Fixing the pension contributions

Each time a Chancellor of the Exchequer makes a Budget speech, he announces various changes that he proposes to make and items he intends to leave unchanged. Parliament debates his proposals and the decisions are eventually made effective in a Finance Act. Among the items it includes are changes in the National Insurance contributions employers and employees are to make. The amounts employers have to pay differ from the employees' contributions and are usually greater.

Noting what the earners contribute

Most of the earners who are aged between 16 and state pension age must pay NI contributions, whether they are employees or self-employed. For employees the contributions depend on the amount of their earnings in relation to lower and upper limits. The limits, as well as the rates of contribution, are set out in the Finance Acts and the contributions are called Class 1 contributions. Employees whose earnings are less than the lower limit do not contribute. Other employees contribute a small percentage of their earnings up to the lower limit and a higher percentage of earnings between the lower and upper limits.

Making the contributions

An employer is responsible for:

* deducting the appropriate contributions from each employee's pay and

* passing them and the employer's own contributions to the Inland Revenue.

Earners who are self-employed must pay Class 2 contributions of the amount fixed for the time being. These entitle them to receive the state pension at the state pension age. If a self-employed person is earning less than a limit currently in force, he or she may claim exemption from liability for Class 2 contributions but will then cease to build up rights to a state pension.

If there have been gaps in an earner's contributions which would prejudice his or her pension entitlement, he or she may make voluntary Class 3 contributions to plug the gaps.

BELONGING TO AN OCCUPATIONAL PENSION SCHEME

In the last half century the number of employers who have set up schemes to provide occupational pensions for their employees has increased greatly. The existence of a good scheme has become one of the principal attractions that many employers have highlighted when advertising job vacancies. But although most people are glad to be able to say that their jobs are pensionable, many of them have only vague ideas about what benefits their schemes will provide for them and their dependants.

Telling employees about their benefits

It is essential for employers to tell their employees their rights and duties under a pension scheme.

It has been normal practice, for many years, for employers to give their employees booklets introducing them to their pension schemes and what they provide. Unfortunately many of these are never read, and others are quickly mislaid.

This has been understandable. Many of the booklets have been far from easy reading. If you are already a member of a scheme, or if you become one, do make sure that you read every handout of this kind and put it in a safe place where you can quickly refer to it.

Making sure that you understand the rules

Don't be put off by difficult language. Ask somebody who is responsible for the scheme to explain it to you. There is nothing to be ashamed of in not understanding the jargon some handouts contain. Ask for it to be put in simple language.

Take equal care of any periodical reports about the scheme that you receive. If they puzzle you, ask for somebody to explain them to you.

Keeping booklets safe

A warning note must be struck here. Some of the explanatory book-lets are brilliantly designed and may even contain cartoons that are intended to illustrate key features of their schemes. That can be an excellent idea. It can make a point highly effectively, but it may contain an unsuspected hazard. Members' children have been known to regard such booklets as comics, and to put them in their toy box.

PARTNERING A MEMBER OF AN OCCUPATIONAL SCHEME

In this book the word 'partner' is used in its residential sense – not to describe a business relationship. In other words, it refers to some-body who lives with you, with or without the formality of a marriage certificate.

Many pension schemes provide benefits payable to widows and other dependent relatives of members, or other people nominated by members. These are mentioned in the appropriate places in this book. Be careful to take account of any that might apply, when seeing where you stand.

CONTRIBUTING TO A PERSONAL PENSION

Are you making maximum permissible contributions to your personal pension? That is a question you should ask yourself each year. And there is the other side of the coin, too. Are you paying more than your earnings permit? You should ask yourself both questions each year. Figure 4 in Chapter 4 will remind you of the limits to what you can contribute.

Have you made any provision for payment of a widow's or wid-ower's pension? Chapter 6 gives details of how you may – and some-times MUST – do this.

Including earnings from various sources

Some people can take earnings from several sources into account, for the purpose of determining how much they can contribute to a personal pension. These earnings may derive from:

- their main employments (in which they belong to no pension scheme)

- second employments that do not clash with their main employments

- sundry odd jobs done in their spare time.

GOING IT ALONE

For some reason – or for no reason that you would acknowledge – you may have steered clear of all the ways of providing yourself with a pension in retirement except making minimum contributions to the state pension. You have not ignored the possibility – or even probability – that you will eventually need to retire. You have put a trivial sum into a building society and invested a few hundred pounds in Ernie. You also have an endowment policy for £1,000 plus bonuses. Your father pushed you into it when you started earning. It will mature when you are 65. You have never thought of taking out additional policies as your income has increased.

Letting time slip by

Your father is no longer there to nag you into doing something about it.

When the time comes for you to retire, you will sell your business. It should raise a few thousand pounds. You may also sell your house and buy a flat. That should realise a reasonable profit to add to the kitty. And you will qualify for the basic state pension, of course.

Surely the time has come for you to take advantage of some of the opportunities you have been missing out on for at least 40 years. Personal pensions have been available since 1956. There is no way that you can retrieve all the tax savings you could have made. But Chapter 5 will show you how you might still qualify for some of them.

RECEIVING A PENSION ALREADY

There are many occupations in which retirement several years before state pension age is common, if not universal. Membership of the armed forces or the police are well-known examples.

People who start to draw pensions at a relatively young age seldom sit back and twiddle their thumbs. They find other employment, on a full-time or part-time basis. Some set up their own businesses. Others become freelance consultants, utilising the skills they have acquired in their previous occupations. Others succeed in careers of which they have no previous experience but which they have always fancied.

Qualifying for further retirement benefits

All of these people can reasonably wish to qualify for a further pension to become payable when their new occupations come to an end. They may qualify for occupational pensions in their new employments: they may prefer or need to arrange for personal pensions. They will, of course, eventually qualify for state pensions.

The one option that is *not* usually available is to discontinue receiving the first pension temporarily and qualify for larger payments when they resume. But there would be nothing to prevent them from accumulating the surplus pension payments in a building society account, or other investment, until they needed them. In the meantime they would receive interest.

CHECKLIST

- Have you a female partner or other close female relative who was born after 5 April 1950?

- If you have, does she realise that she will not be able to draw her state pension until later than her 60th birthday?

- Do you belong to an occupational pension scheme?

- If you do:
  - Can you lay your hands on the explanatory booklet?
  - Do you understand it?
  - If not, have you asked somebody to explain it?

- Are you contributing to a personal pension?

- If you are, do you keep your contributions up to the maximum permitted?

- Are you already drawing a pension from an employment with an unusually early retirement age, and launched on a second career?

- If you are, have you also started:
  - investing part of each month's pension?
  - paying part of your current earnings into a personal pension?

2
Contrasting the Benefits Provided

'What am I going to get out of it?' That is the first question that automatically springs to mind when the subject of pensions crops up. To some extent the answer must be, 'Wait and see'. Who knows when the benefits will become payable? Life is so uncertain. But it is possible to indicate the bases on which the various ways of providing retirement benefits operate.

QUALIFYING FOR A STATE PENSION

We have already seen how long people have to wait to qualify to receive a pension, but passing the appropriate milestone is not the only requirement.

Identifying qualifying years
For the purpose of deciding whether somebody has chalked up enough contributions to qualify for a pension one must see how many qualifying years there are during his or her 'working life'.

Your working life begins at the start of the tax year in which you reach your 16th birthday and finishes at the end of the tax year before the one in which you reach state pension age.

A qualifying year is a tax year during which you have received, or are treated as having received, qualifying earnings of at least 52 times the lower earnings limit for that year. (Earnings of married women and widows on which they have paid reduced-rate Class 1 contributions do not count as qualifying earnings.)

Being entitled to credits
In some situations, where there is an involuntary non-payment of contributions, a credit for them will be given. This applies

principally where a person is receiving:

- Invalid Care Allowance
- Disability Working Allowance
- Jobseeker's Allowance
- Severe Disablement Allowance
- Incapacity Benefit
- Approved Training.

Also, men are now credited with earnings for the tax years in which they reach age 60, and subsequently, until the tax year before they reach age 65. From 6 April 2010 this arrangement will also apply to women, with the substitution of 'pensionable age' for 'age 65'. **NB.** The credit does *not* apply for any week in which the person is liable to pay Class 2 contributions, by reason of self-employment, or for any year in which he or she is abroad for 182 days or more.

Achieving full pension entitlement

To qualify for a full basic pension, you need to have qualifying years for approximately 90 per cent of your working life. The following table gives the formula for calculating the relationship between your working life and qualifying years, more precisely.

Length of working life	Number of qualifying years needed
41 years of more	Length of working life minus five
31–40 years	Length of working life minus four

Noting a married woman's pension

A married woman whose qualifying years would entitle her to a retirement pension at pension age if she were not married is still entitled to that pension.

A married woman who has no such entitlement is entitled to a retirement pension equal to about 60 per cent of her husband's pension and payable from his pension age. But if she has qualifying years of her own which entitle her to a pension smaller than the one mentioned in the previous sentence, she can have the difference made up to her from her husband's pension age. An example may make this easier to grasp.

Example

When Mary reaches pension age, her qualifying years entitle her to a pension of only £29 a week. When John, her husband, reaches pension age, his qualifying years entitle him to a full pension of £60 a week. If Mary had no pension of her own, she would be entitled to a pension of £36 a week, based on John's qualifying years. Because she is already entitled to receive a pension in respect of her own qualifying years, she cannot receive the £36 a week. However, her existing £29 a week is increased to £36 a week. (Please note that these figures are given solely for purposes of illustration and are not actual figures.)

Dealing with graduated and State Earnings-Related Pensions

Until now we have been dealing with basic pensions. There are two additional state pensions you may need to know about.

The first is the **graduated pension** that was built up between 1961 and 1975 for people who earned more than £9 a week. When the government of the day discontinued the build-up in 1975 the benefits were frozen, but since 1978 they have been inflation-proofed. The Department of Social Security has maintained records of people's entitlement to these benefits so that they may be paid when the basic pension becomes payable. Few people receive more than £3 a week in respect of the graduated pension.

The other additional state pension is that provided by the **State Earnings-Related Pension Scheme** (SERPS). For people who were then employees, this started to build up additional benefits from 6 April 1978 unless somebody took action to prevent it. The preventive action would be either the employer contracting out an occupational pension scheme or an employee contracting out a personal pension.

The addition made to the state pension by SERPS is based on the employee's earnings between the lower and upper earnings limits for National Insurance contributions since 6 April 1978.

UNDERSTANDING SCHEME MEMBERS' BENEFITS

In the last 50 years, people who have designed occupational pension schemes have experimented with various patterns of benefits for the members. Their experience has led them to concentrate on two basic types of scheme, but there is plenty of scope for fine tuning within each of those types. No useful purpose would be served by examining the other types that have fallen into the discard pile.

Final salary schemes

These are schemes in which a member's pension is defined by some such formula as 'One eightieth of the member's final annual salary for each complete year of service with the company'. For achieving simplicity of their objective, these schemes are probably understood and appreciated most readily by the majority of the members. If a member knows that the pension will be a given proportion of one's rate of pay immediately before retirement, that should be easy to grasp.

But if a member's earning capacity wanes in the final year or two, should that reduce the pension of somebody who has given 30 or 40 years of loyal service?

Defining final annual salary

A skilfully drafted definition of 'final annual salary' can cover such a situation satisfactorily. For example, it might be defined as 'the highest actual earnings of the member during 12 consecutive calendar months in the 60 months that immediately precede the member's retirement date'.

On the other hand, since the employer has paid something like half of the NI contributions for a member, would it be reasonable to reduce the amount of the occupational pension, to take account of this? Those contributions are part of the justification the Department of Social Security has for paying the member's state pension.

Agreeing terms

Those are only two of the factors an employer may need to take into account. The employees and their representatives may point out others. There is scope for considerable variation in the way a member's pension entitlement is defined. Whatever formula is adopted, the definition should be precise and clear.

Money purchase schemes

Instead of defining benefits by reference to earnings and length of service, this type of scheme establishes a basis on which the employer and each member contribute to the cost of the benefits. For each member the employer and the member might contribute x per cent and y per cent respectively of the member's earnings. The contributions in respect of each member would be invested separately – notionally, at least – and the build-up of his or her fund recorded.

In practice it would be uneconomic to segregate each member's fund. The charges for handling small investments are proportionally much higher than those for larger amounts. So scheme members benefit from the bulk dealings in investments for all the members of a scheme.

Paying benefits
When benefits become payable, the records show how much stands to the credit of the member concerned. Appropriate investments are sold to provide that amount of cash. This is applied to set up benefits in respect of the member on the basis laid down in the rules of the scheme.

On the face of it, this is a more hit-or-miss way of providing benefits than a final salary scheme achieves. Many members may feel less aware of what pensions they are heading for, than under a final salary scheme.

However, there are people who prefer money purchase. In particular high-fliers may think that it provides a more certain basis for passing the value of their benefits from one scheme to another as they change their jobs and soar higher and higher.

Receiving lump sums in lieu of pension
There has been a tradition stretching back into the 19th century that an employee who retires on pension is allowed to receive an immediate lump sum instead of part of his or her pension. This option is normally included in the terms of both final salary and money purchase schemes.

PERMITTING PERSONAL PENSIONS

Before a sympathetic Chancellor introduced tax concessions to assist the marketing of personal pensions, self-employed people were at a disadvantage compared with their own employees. Employees whose employers had not set up pension schemes for them were missing out, too.

Having two or more jobs
The new opportunities also interested people who had pensionable jobs but had additional earnings from work they did 'outside office hours'. These included not only clerks who earned extra money by stocking supermarket shelves in the evenings but also surgeons or physicians who were consultants in NHS hospitals for x hours a week and attended private patients in their free time.

Untapped moonlighting

One way or another, there are hundreds of thousands of people who could benefit from using part of their spare-time earnings to pay for personal pensions. The proportion who do this may be fairly small. The people with such additional earnings are likely to be largely unknown to the people who market personal pensions. That could be an important factor, because personal pensions are usually sold rather than bought. And it may never occur to a perennial moonlighter that having a pension from only one employment is a poor sequel to having two regular sources of earnings.

Noting necessary basis

In any comparison between personal pensions and occupational pensions it is quickly apparent that a personal pension cannot be a final salary type of arrangement. It is essentially a money purchase arrangement.

The option of receiving a cash sum in place of part of the pension is included in the terms of a personal pension arrangement.

ENJOYING FLEXIBILITY OF PENSION AGE

Physically and mentally, people are not created equal. And they experience differing circumstances at home, at school and in their careers. Hardly surprisingly a standard retiring age is far from suitable for all of them. Some die without reaching that age, some stagger over the finishing line like an out-of-form marathon runner, and some resent the suggestion that the time has come for them to put their feet up. They want to postpone retiring for as long as possible. How much flexibility of retirement age do the various types of pension provision offer?

State pensions

As many people have discovered, in recent years, if one is laid off before state pension age, one has to wait until that age to become entitled to the state pension. (Someone who has to quit a job early because of ill health may qualify for a disability benefit, but that is not a pension.)

Someone who, when reaching pension age, wishes to defer receiving the state pension may do so for up to five years. He or she may have substantial earnings from one source or another and want to keep down the income tax liability. During the period of deferment the amount of the pension will be increased by about 7.5 per cent each year, *ie* about 37.5 per cent for five years.

Chopping and changing

Also, when payment of a pension has begun, a pensioner may decide to postpone drawing it, for a while. That is permissible, but chopping and changing is not allowed. Once payment recommences, it cannot be postponed again. And a male pensioner whose wife is drawing a pension based on his contributions cannot postpone his pension without her consent, because payment of her pension would be postponed, too.

Flexible occupational schemes

Each scheme has a normal pension age. This may be any age between 50 and 75 but is usually either 60 or 65. Other ages may be used where the nature of the occupation is such that those limits are clearly inappropriate. For example professional sportsmen's playing careers normally end before they reach 50. Even Sir John Berry Hobbs retired from the cricket field at 53, and he was clearly exceptional. Sir Stanley Matthews hung up his football boots at 40.

It has been accepted in several cases that a particular scheme for professional footballers can have a normal pension age of 35, but the Inland Revenue does not have a list enshrining such an age for them. If a member wishes to retire before normal pension age, this may be allowed if the member's age is not less than 50. However, if the retirement is because of a decline in physical or mental health which seriously reduces the member's ability to do the job, the minimum age does not apply.

Retiring early

Normally if a member retires early, the amount of the pension is reduced. This is to take account of the shortening of the period in which the pension has been paid for and the possible increase in the number of years during which payment of the pension will be made.

Because of the streamlining of staff and other changes in the structure of businesses, many long-serving employees have been persuaded to take early retirement during recent years. In most cases the rules of their employers' pension schemes have permitted payment of a pension to commence early, at an age not less than 50. And in some cases employers have been happy to foot the bill for increasing the pensions to what they would have been at normal pension age.

Staying on

Less frequent than requests to be allowed to retire early are enquiries about the possibility of being allowed to soldier on for a while, when normal pension age arrives. If it suits the employer's book, this may be agreed to. However, in the rare event that the suggested extension of service would take it beyond the employee's 75th birthday, special arrangements need to be made. It would be inappropriate to describe them here.

Personal pensions

Nowhere in the world of pensions is there greater flexibility than in a personal pension. Within the limits that legislation imposes:

- a person's contributions may vary from year to year

- drawing a pension may commence at any age between 50 and 75

- easing into retirement by successive tranches of pension is possible.

  An example will clarify that facility.

Example
Richard draws an income from each of three directorships. He pays the appropriate percentage of his income from company A into one personal pension, the same percentage of his income from company B into another personal pension and that percentage of his income from company C into a third personal pension. On his 65th birthday he resigns his directorship with company A and starts to draw his first personal pension. On his 70th and 75th birthdays he deals similarly with companies B and C and starts to draw his second and third personal pensions respectively. He has progressively reduced both his working week and his earnings but increased his leisure and his retirement income.

PROVIDING DEATH BENEFITS

In *Richard II*, Shakespeare wrote, 'Let's choose executors and talk of wills'. That could be wise advice to anybody who had made no move in that direction. It would be even better advice if it included making wills. Talking is not enough. At least the state scheme and many employers' pension schemes give some thought to what happens to dependants when a member dies.

State pension scheme

Apart from widows' pensions, which are described later in this chapter, the state scheme makes little provision of death benefits. There is, however, a single lump-sum **widow's payment** of £1,000 that may be made. This is primarily payable to women who are less than 60 years old when their husbands die.

The £1,000 may also be claimed by a widow who had reached the age of 60 when her husband died if:

- EITHER he was under 65 when he died

- OR he had reached that age but deferred drawing his state pension.

Occupational pension schemes

For many years it has been the practice of most occupational schemes to make a lump-sum payment when a member dies while in the employer's service. This may be a fixed amount, but it may be or include a refund of any contributions the member has made.

It is also a common practice for schemes to make a lump-sum payment if a member dies in retirement, within five years of the commencement of pension payments. This often amounts to the balance of five years' pension payments. Instead it may be slightly less, to allow for the fact that the money is being paid before those payments would have been due.

Dealing with the lump sum

Sometimes such a lump sum is payable to someone nominated by the member to receive it. But the rules of many schemes give trustees discretion to choose the beneficiary (see Figure 2 and Chapter 4). The rules then usually prescribe the area within which the trustees may choose. The primary purpose of the discretion is to reduce the risk of the lump sum being subject to Inheritance Tax.

If you are a member of a scheme for which the rules make any provision for the lump sum to be paid to somebody nominated by the member

- either automatically
- or subject to the approval of the trustees,

you would be wise to make a nomination and make sure that the trustees know it exists.

'The trustees shall make payment of any lump sum becoming payable on the death of a member to such of the following parties as the trustees in their absolute discretion shall choose, namely the member's spouse, children, siblings, next of kin, personal representatives, and any person nominated in writing by the member to receive the payment. Provided that, if the trustees have not exercised that discretion within two years of the member's death, they shall make payment immediately to the personal representatives.'

The purposes of using such a wording are:

- to avoid the lump sum's passing automatically on death and consequently being taxed

- to allow the trustees to ignore any nomination made by the member if they know that circumstances had so changed since it was made that it ceased representing the wishes of the member before he or she died

- to ensure that payment is made without excessive delay.

Fig. 2. Lump sum payable on the death of a member: Example of a possible wording for a scheme rule relating to its disposal.

- You could place it in a sealed envelope, addressed to the trustees and marked 'Not to be opened except on the death of . . . . .'.

Remember to:

- add your name

- make a new nomination if the nominee dies or falls out of favour.

Personal pensions

Usually a lump sum representing the contributions made is payable if the owner of a personal pension dies before the pension becomes payable. He or she can also direct, when arranging the personal pension, that a life assurance shall provide a specified sum to supplement the refund of contributions if he or she dies before payment of the pension is due to start.

PROVIDING PENSIONS FOR DEPENDANTS

An immediate lump sum to pay funeral expenses and any outstanding bills may be the most pressing need when somebody has died. But soon the loss of the earnings of the deceased may become a major hardship. A pension to replace at least part of those earnings would be a great boon. Where could it come from?

State pension scheme

The person needing this kind of financial support most is usually the widow. If she is between 55 and 64 years old and has not begun to draw the state retirement pension, she should receive a widow's basic pension. If her late husband had not made full qualifying contributions, the amount of the pension would be reduced unless he died of an industrial accident or disease. In that event there would be no reduction in the widow's pension.

In respect of the husband's earnings since April 1978 there would be an addition to the state pension, but this would be halved for any period during which he had been contracted out of SERPS. (The occupational or personal pension that qualified him for the contracting out should also, of course, provide a pension at least as large as the remaining half of the addition to the state pension.)

If the widow was at least 45 but not yet 55 when her husband died, she would be entitled to a reduced pension. The percentage reduction would depend on her age at the time of his death: it would not change subsequently.

Helping widowed mothers

There is an additional income that is not called a pension but is payable to widows who have dependent children. It is called a 'widowed mother's allowance' and is payable to a widow who does not qualify for a widow's pension but has dependent children. In this context they cease to be regarded as dependent at 16 (or 19 if they are in full-time education).

A widow's pension ceases if she remarries before age 60. And if she lives with a man as his wife, the pension is suspended as long as the co-habitation continues.

Occupational pension schemes

This is an area where a money purchase scheme could be less than exciting unless steps were taken to provide for reasonable payments on early deaths. There would be a derisory amount in the kitty if a member died after being in the scheme for a few months only and the death benefit was a refund of the member's contributions.

If such a scheme is to guard against such a contingency it needs some form of guarantee for dependants' pensions, such as life assurance cover, at least during the members' early years. To continue it throughout their working years could be even wiser.

Insuring death benefits

With life assurance back-up, a money purchase scheme and a final salary scheme are each able to provide dependants' pensions, whether a member dies while still an employee or in retirement. Chapter 6 deals with important criteria a scheme must satisfy in connection with such benefits and others. But it is desirable to mention, at this point, that the people who are responsible for running a scheme need to know the identity, age and sex of a dependant to whom a pension may become payable. The cost of providing pensions of £x a year each for a 20-year-old woman and a 40-year-old man are very different.

Although dependants' pensions are most frequently payable to widows and widowers of members – and increasingly to members' partners – they are sometimes provided for other people who are financially dependent on a member. For example, one might be provided for a physically or mentally handicapped son or daughter or, on a temporary basis, for a child until age 18 or 21.

Unlike state pensions, occupational scheme widows' pensions often do not cease if a widow remarries, nor is payment of a widow's pension suspended if she starts to live with a man as husband and wife. Most employers and trustees prefer not to need to concern themselves with checking on intimate details of widows' lives.

Personal pensions

A personal pension arrangement may include insurance of a lump sum payable by a life office if the owner of the personal pension dies before his or her pension is due to commence. If the lump sum becomes payable, the person who is entitled to receive it may use it to buy an annuity for a dependant of the deceased, payable for the remainder of the dependant's life.

If the owner of the personal pension survives until payment of that pension is due to commence, the fund that has been accumulated to pay for it may be used to buy an annuity either:

(i)   payable during the remainder of the owner's life, or

(ii) payable during the joint lifetime of the owner and a dependant, and continuing during the remaining lifetime of the survivor, or

(iii) payable as in (ii) but reducing * on the first death.

*For a given purchase price, (iii) will provide a larger initial annuity than (ii). The most usual reductions are 50 per cent or $33\frac{1}{3}$ per cent.

CHECKLIST

• Do all the 'ifs and buts' of the state pensions muddle you? That need not worry you. There is no need for you to try to remember them. The Department of Social Security will tell you what you are entitled to, when the time comes.

• Do you have a second source of earnings, outside your normal working hours?

• If you do, have you a personal pension policy, to which you pay part of those earnings?

• If not, you might be wise to save some of the income tax you have to pay on those earnings.

• Does your occupational pension scheme pay a lump sum death benefit if you die before you reach pension age?

• If so, can you nominate to whom you would wish the trustees to pay it?

• If you can, have you made a written nomination and given it to the trustees?

• If you haven't, **you should do it immediately**.

3
Discovering how Benefits are Paid for

You have noticed that people who retire from where you work always seem happy when they have a quiet celebration on their last day. You are confident that this is not induced by alcohol. You believe that, like them, you will be entitled to receive a pension when you retire, but you would like to know more, even if it is only dotting the i's and crossing the t's. It would be most unfortunate if you found that you had been misled.

The disappearance of Robert Maxwell may have sown a seed of doubt in your mind. It encouraged many people to ask questions.

'Are we really living in cloud-cuckoo-land?'

'Shall we wake up, one day, to find that all the talk about pensions is a lot of eyewash?'

'Perhaps even the old age pension is on its way out. One way or another, there's been a lot of mucking about with pensions in the last ten or 15 years.'

The then government accepted that there was scope for things to go wrong. On 19 July 1995 'an Act to amend the law about pensions and for connected purposes' received the Royal Assent. It became part of the law of the land. This chapter and those that follow will answer many of the questions. They will point out how the Pensions Act 1995 has increased the security of the pensions you and your friends and family have been told that you and they will receive.

UNDERSTANDING FISCAL RESOURCING OF STATE PENSIONS

What a horrible heading! What does it mean?

It refers to the way that government-controlled finances are organised. In other words, 'How do the National Insurance contributions of you and your employer pay for your state pension, when the time comes for you to draw it?'

You may have a mental picture of those contributions being like a stream of cocoa beans, milk and sugar pouring into one end of a massive machine, and a bar of pensions chocolate emerging at the other end. Forget it! The contributions are only part of the sum your employer sends to the government funds, each month. It relates also to NI contributions for other employees, income tax deducted from their pay and yours, and many other taxes and excise duties.

Creating a reservoir of money

NI contributions are not segregated from all the other money that the government collects, one way or another. Money from all parts of the nation goes to swell an enormous fund with which the government pays its bills. Those bills are not only for pensions but also for a thousand and one other matters that the government has to pay for.

It may seem as if you lose track of your money as soon as it is paid over to the Collector of Taxes. Look at it from a different angle. If you have a car, you have to buy a road fund licence, and we all know that this is not used specifically to build and maintain roads for you to drive your car on. Neither is the fuel tax on the petrol or diesel oil you put in the tank of your car. But the government does use large sums of money to finance road building and road maintenance.

It could be said that when you pay for a new tax disc for your car, you buy a right to drive the car on public highways. The government provides the highways.

Tapping the reservoir

In a similar way, your NI contributions buy a right for you and your dependants to receive state scheme benefits when you and they qualify to receive them. The government finds the money to pay for those benefits, when they become due, from that enormous fund. It is a fund to which you and millions of other people have each contributed a minuscule part.

Meanwhile the NI contributions that have been paid by you or on your behalf are duly recorded. The records are evidence of your eventual entitlement to receive benefits.

FINDING MONEY TO PAY FOR OCCUPATIONAL SCHEME BENEFITS

Gone are the days when an employer assumed that a retiring employee had put something aside to supplement the old age pension, and sent him on his way with a marble clock or a gold pocket watch as a memento. The timepiece may have ticked away all the passing hours of the rest of the retired employee's life. It provided no material resources to brighten those hours.

Nowadays people expect something better. The majority of them qualify for a pension. Some of the pensions may be little more than a pittance. But many enable the pensioner to continue to enjoy a reasonably comfortable standard of living.

Paying a pension as an expense

Doubtless there are still some private employers who ease gardeners and other domestic employees into retirement by paying them wages that are effectively pensions. These employers continue paying those ageing retainers in spite of their working hours being rapidly reduced to nil. Their continuing weekly or monthly payments are made in appreciation of services rendered, just like many other people's non-contributory pensions.

The number of commercial employers in the United Kingdom who still pay pensions as current expenses must be very small. The incentives for setting up a modern pension scheme make continuing any such method unattractive in the UK.

But there are several groups of people whose pensions derive from the current income of one employer – the government. They include pensioners from the Civil Service and the armed forces, retired judges, former Members of Parliament and Cabinet ministers, and various other groups of people who have received salaries – directly or indirectly – from government funds. The terms of the pension schemes for *some* of them require members to contribute to the cost. Their contributions are deducted from their pay.

Between them the members of these groups make up a large proportion of the working population. Unlike commercial employers, their employers do not need to make a profit, each year, in order to stay in business.

Building up a pension fund

Optimism is an excellent trait for anybody to possess, but your income in your later years needs to be based on certainty, as far as possible. No employer or employee can rule out the possibility of a catastrophe, but the odds against one occurring should be reduced as far as possible. A sensible businessman insures against such risks as fire, accident and theft. If he also builds up a reserve fund clearly earmarked for providing pensions for employees, those employees might assume that they should be all right.

Checking the size of the fund

To make sure that he gets his sums right, he employs an expert to estimate how much he needs to put into the fund. It must be large enough to pay all the benefits when they become due. He invests the fund prudently, after taking knowledgeable advice.

He has taken the steps he considers necessary to provide for his employees' needs in retirement. Now he can concentrate on running the business so that he and they will earn enought to live on, while they are working.

That is fine, as far as it goes, but does it go far enough? What will happen if – in spite of all his care and precautions – the business becomes insolvent and the creditors have a liquidator appointed? The liquidator will have a duty to seize all the assets of the business. Unfortunately the pension fund will be one of them.

Erecting a legal fence round the fund

To guard against such a fate befalling the fund, it must be put into trust while the business is solvent. A trust is a legal arrangement by which property (in this case the pension fund) is held by one or more trustees for the benefit of defined beneficiaries (in this case the employees).

The document that creates the trust spells out the terms of the trust and appoints one or more trustees to be responsible for dealing with the pension fund in accordance with those terms. Even if the employer is the only trustee, the liquidator cannot touch the fund. The employer holds it on behalf of the employees. Neither he nor anybody else can deal with it otherwise than as the terms of the trust document provide.

Chapter 4 deals in more detail with the appointment and responsibilities of trustees. For the moment it is enough to say that they watch over the assets of the trust and see that they are used to pay the right benefits to the right people at the right time.

Including members as contributors

Should an employer bear the whole cost of a pension scheme for the employees or should they have to contribute? The question has been asked many times. Both employers and employees have argued fervently about the advantages and disadvantages of contributory and non-contributory schemes.

When occupational pensions were far less common than they are today, many employees preferred a contributory scheme because they could take a refund of their contributions if they moved from one job to another. When jobs were plentiful, it was not unknown for people to move from one employer to another solely to get the refund. There was even at least one town in England where employees of two adjacent factories often moved from one factory to the other when they wanted a deposit for a new washing machine and moved back when they wanted another deposit for another major purchase. They gave no thought to the long-term benefits they were sacrificing by their activities.

Enforcing preservation of benefits

Since April 1975 there has been severe limitation of the scope for refunds of contributions on leaving service. More recently the scope has been limited still further. If a departing employee has been a member of a contributory scheme for less than two years, the scheme has a right to return the member's own contributions, less 20 per cent tax. But the member **does not** have a right to **demand** a refund. (Additional considerations arise if the scheme has been contracted out – see Chapter 7.)

Employment opportunities have changed, too. Pension schemes have figured more and more in the remuneration packages employers have offered to attract recruits of the right calibre.

Some employers believe that people take more interest in their pension rights if they are contributing to the cost of the scheme. Financially it is virtually immaterial to the employer whether the scheme is contributory or non-contributory. If it is to be contributory, the employees will expect to get a pay increase to cover their contributions so the employer will give the pay increase with one hand, take it away with the other, and put it into the pension fund.

Making additional voluntary contributions

Whether a scheme is contributory or non-contributory, one or more of the members may wish to obtain larger benefits at retirement than the scheme usually provides. The laws and regulations relating to pension schemes lay down certain limits for the benefits that may be provided. Chapter 6 deals with these.

A scheme may provide benefits that are smaller than those limits would permit. Indeed few – if any – schemes provide every possible benefit up to the limit. The documents that give details of the scheme may not set out those limits. Nor may they mention other permissible benefits that the scheme does not normally provide.

If you wish to make additional voluntary contributions (AVCs) to the scheme to which you belong, the people in charge of the scheme must (with a few minor exceptions) be willing to accept them, for the purpose of increasing the benefits within the permissible limits. However, the terms they offer, using the scheme's usual investment provider, may not appeal to you. You may be able to achieve your objective more satisfactorily by means of free standing AVCs (FSAVCs) made to another provider. In this context an 'investment provider' is one of the organisations for managing pension fund investments that are mentioned in Chapter 4.

PAYING FOR PERSONAL PENSIONS

Tax advantages for the forerunners of today's personal pensions were introduced in 1956. They were called 'self-employed retirement annuities'. The innovation was part of a package of changes that was made to harmonise the tax treatment of various ways of providing retirement incomes. Until then there was no tax-friendly route by which earners who were self-employed could provide pensions for themselves. People who were described as 'controlling directors of director-controlled companies' suffered the same disadvantage. In general these were earners who owned most of the shares in private limited companies, and often did all or much of the work themselves.

The Finance Act 1956 removed the disadvantage. It permitted these two types of people to use a percentage of their earnings to pay for personal pensions and enjoy tax advantages comparable to those allowed to members of occupational pension schemes. It also allowed employees whose employers had made no pension provision for them to pay for personal pensions.

Subsequent legislation has widened the area to which earners may direct their pension contributions and made various other broadly beneficial changes that are mentioned and explained in later chapters.

SAVING TO GO IT ALONE

Why choose this route to having enough to support yourself and any partner when the time for retirement arrives? Admittedly having a nest-egg put aside for such an occasion has a long tradition, but most people look for something else, nowadays.

Perhaps you have bought a house, with the help of a mortgage, and should have paid off the loan, barring accidents, before retirement arrives. By then you will probably no longer need as large a house. Moving into a smaller house or a flat should release a cash sum that you could invest to provide a retirement income.

Backing your judgement

Maybe you have a flair for choosing equity shares that are likely to appreciate more rapidly than the Stock Exchange indexes. Or maybe you know that you are sole beneficiary under the will of a relation who started accumulating top class investments 70 years ago. At his age, he must surely shuffle off this mortal coil within the next ten years. But are you sure that he has had no need to sell many of his investments to pay for his accommodation in the pricey nursing home where he is living?

Selling your business

You may have an investment that you feel more entitled to rely on than any of those other examples. You have your own business. You built it up yourself, and its profits have grown much faster than the cost of living. The premises are worth a large sum, the business is in excellent shape, and the goodwill should command a tidy sum. But are you sure that your valuation of these assets matches their true worth?

Extending your horizons

Whatever justification you may have had for deciding to go it alone, in the past, might you be wise *now* to have at least one other string to your bow?

Have you ever given serious thought to investing in one or more unit trusts? You will appreciate that the price of their units can go down, as well as up. That may not worry you too much, if you are unlikely to need to get your hands on cash in a hurry. If you choose a growth fund, with a view to having something in reserve when you are approaching retirement, it may fill the bill.

Choosing a trust

Which trust should you choose? There are so many in the market.

You could start your search by studying either or both of two magazines – *Money Management* and *Planned Savings*. Both of them publish helpful surveys of past performances of various funds. These may not be infallible guides to future performance, but they are better than using a pin.

Another possible investment that you might consider is a traditional with profit endowment assurance with a life assurance company. That is a policy that promises payment of a basic sum assured plus accruing bonuses on, say, your planned retirement date or your previous death. It was what people used to make provision for their retirement before personal pensions arrived. The life office adds bonuses at regular intervals. Once they have been added, the bonuses can't be taken away. And there is no requirement for you to take any part of the proceeds at your retirement age in the form of a pension, as there would be with a personal pension.

Buying an annuity

You could, of course, use all or part of the money to buy an annuity, if you so wished. Part only of each instalment of the annuity would be taxable as income. The remainder would be regarded, for tax purposes, as a return of part of the capital sum you had invested in the annuity.

You might also consider putting money into another traditional and straightforward investment – the National Savings Certificate. The number of issues of these inexpensive units that have been marketed is evidence of their popularity. They are:

* available in a range of convenient numbers of units to suit all pockets

* tax free

* easily cashed, when necessary

* convertible into later issues, when their terms expire.

POINTS TO CONSIDER

1. Successive governments pay state pensions out of income: commercial employers do not. Why? Is it because:
   – they have fewer employees?
   – their income fluctuates from year to year?
   – they have no power to raise taxes from the community?

2. How does having a pension fund controlled by trustees help the members of the pension scheme?

3. Why might you be wise to make additional voluntary contributions (AVCs) to your employer's pension scheme?

4. If your employer has no occupational pension scheme, how would you benefit if you took out a personal pension?

4
Assessing the Security of Benefits

'Next to the Bank of England, and as safe!' That was the slogan of an insurance company many years ago. Both the Bank and the company are still in business, so the slogan was justified. But how does one assess the safety of a pension scheme?

PROVIDING STATE PENSIONS FROM TAXES

When the then government established the welfare state, soon after the ending of World War II, many people were disgusted by the way they were treated in connection with voluntary contributions they had made under the previous system. Under it compulsory contributions had been payable for employees earning less than a modest amount. If people's earnings rose above that amount, their compulsory contributions stopped but they were allowed to continue contributing, on a voluntary basis, so as to qualify for a state pension at age 65.

When the new state scheme came into being, the complaint of people who had made such voluntary contributions was that those contributions had disappeared into the kitty, without so much as a 'thank you'. The people who had made them received no addition to their state pensions, in respect of them, under the new scheme.

The number of people who lost out was small compared with the millions who gained under the new system, but their loss rankled with them for many years. Governments of each of the major parties succeeded one another at Westminster and ignored the complaint. Most of the victims have now died.

Learning from experience
To quote this example of an injustice that deprived a minority of the population of their rights is not to suggest that people who are currently making NI contributions will miss out on their state pensions, one day. On the other hand, it would be wrong to overlook

the possibility that a Chancellor of the Exchequer who was strapped for cash might make subtle adjustments to the allocations of resources to the various government departments, so as to balance the books. There would then be winners and losers. As the late Lord Wilson said, in a different context, 'One man's pay rise is another man's price rise'.

Looking ahead

One problem is certain to arise during the next 25 years, and the three main political parties in the UK all recognise this. The average age at which people retire is going down. The average age at which young people finish full-time education is going up. As a result of these two trends, the ratio of earners to non-earners is going down. Also more people are living into their 80s and 90s than in earlier generations. That reduces the ratio further. How are fewer earners going to cope with paying for the state pensions of more pensioners? And will occupational pension schemes encounter the same sort of problem? If they do, how will they handle it? That is a question that will need an answer in a later section of this chapter.

PAYING OCCUPATIONAL PENSIONS OUT OF PROFITS

The profits that a business makes today derive, in part, from the skill and effort of former employees who have now retired. Nobody could justly begrudge those people's sharing in the continuing prosperity of the business. But by the same tokens, if the business suffers losses as a consequence of the incompetence and laziness of retired former employees, they should share in the losses. On balance employees would almost certainly prefer to rule a line across the page when they retire, and let bygones be bygones, the good ones as well as the bad.

On the other hand if an employer promises to pay a pension to a departing employee, he or she expects the employer to honour the promise. If the business is flourishing, the employer may have no hesitation in making such a promise and the employee may be equally confident in accepting it.

The fortunes of even the most efficient businesses fluctuate. Even if their years' results never dip into the red, businesses have good years and not such good years. In the latter an employer might well regret having promised a pension to a retired employee.

Studying a case

Consider the case of George and Ernest, father and son, who are the directors of a private limited company which has made steady progress for many years. A few months before Alan retired, four years ago, George and Ernest promised to pay him a pension of £x a year. The following year the business did well and they paid Alan a small bonus, in addition to his pension. The next year they increased the bonus by more, and at the end of the third year they repeated the previous year's bonus.

The fourth year was less profitable for the company. George and Ernest spent one evening discussing what to do about Alan's pension. They had no serious qualms about continuing it and the same amount of bonus for another twelve months but decided to discuss the subject more fully after George had visited Alan and put him in the picture.

Analysing the directors' problem

George and Ernest have struck a snag. It all looked plain sailing. They had assumed that, because they were the only shareholders in their private company, there would be no difficulties in Alan's receiving his pension for as long as he lived. It was reasonable to assume that Ernest, at least, would survive him and honour the promise. The company was making good profits, so what risks were they running? They regarded Alan as almost being one of the family. The last thing they wanted to do was let him down.

FUNDING OCCUPATIONAL PENSION BENEFITS

Ernest suggested that they might discharge their responsibility for finding the money to pay a pension to Alan on each anniversary of his retirement by buying an annuity for him from a life assurance company. It would entail paying the company a sum several times as large as the annual amount of the annuity. It was a pity that they had waited as long as this before giving the subject adequate consideration.

If they had wanted to provide pensions for more employees, George and Ernest might have investigated the subject sooner and realised that the only satisfactory way for an employer to provide pensions for employees is to have the cost covered for each employee before retirement arrives. In other words there must be an accumulated fund that is large enough to cover:

- the cost of the immediate pension for Jack, who is now retiring

- a sum which, when added to by regular adequate additions* will cover the cost of every other employee's pension, when he or she retires.

*The adequate additions will be calculated by an actuary – a specialist mathematician who is skilled in quoting the amounts required to achieve the objective. To do this, he or she needs to know full details of:

- the membership of the pension scheme
- the intended benefits
- the investments.

Defining two words

Before we go any further, it would be as well to clarify the meaning of two words that crop up in this book. For our purposes, 'pension' means a series of payments made to a retired person, or to the widow(er) of that person, by either the former employer or the state; 'annuity' means a contract between a life assurance company and an employer by which the life office promises – in return for receiving a lump sum from the employer – to make payments equal to pension payments the employer has promised. The life office quotes terms of the contract based on the assumption that enough pensioners will die young to pay for those who survive to a ripe old age.

INVESTING THE FUNDS

What kind of investments does one expect a pension fund to hold, and who chooses them? In general terms, it could be said that they should be:

- safe
- profitable
- easy to sell without loss.

The last feature becomes less important if the employer's business is expanding and the ages of the employees are well spread. The income of the fund, from current contributions and investment dividends and interest, is then likely to be more than large enough to pay the benefits that are falling due for the older members.

Obtaining investment advice

One would hardly expect the Georges and Ernests of the world to know enough about the market to be able to select the most suitable stocks and shares. And picking the right moment to sell the shares of PQR plc and buy those of XYZ plc is a task for a specialist. That will be somebody whose energies are concentrated on knowing the market. He or she will have a flair for grasping the significance of the day's news, assessing the effect that the death of Smith or the appointment of Jones is likely to have on the fortunes of JKL plc, and recommending appropriate action regarding the company's shares.

A large company with 100,000 members in its pension scheme might well employ such a person as manager of the scheme. A smaller company may engage a skilled investment adviser as a consultant who also acts in a similar capacity for other companies.

Delegating investment management

Another arrangement that may appeal to an employer is to call on the expertise of a financial institution such as a merchant bank or a life assurance company. Each of them has investment specialists on its staff. The bank or life office may assign either an individual or a team to manage the pension fund. A fee to recoup the relevant salaries will be paid by the employer.

An important feature of successful fund management is having a good spread of investments. The traditional philosophy of not having all one's eggs in the same basket applies. To be more precise, one should alter the wording to, 'Don't put your eggs in too few baskets'. The guiding principle is to avoid suffering a severe drop in value of a significant part of the pension fund. Opinions differ as to what constitutes a significant part of a fund.

Spreading the risks

The larger a fund is, the wider the spread of its investments can be. This fact encourages some life assurance companies to operate pooled managed funds. They enable small, and not-so-small, investors to spread their funds over a wider range of securities than they could hope to encompass alone. Such a fund is very much like a unit trust. Pension schemes hand over their cash to the managers of the fund. They use the cash to buy a spread of investments for the pooled fund. This is chosen in a way that is intended to give a reasonable prospect of the fund's maintaining its value. Fluctuations in the values of the securities held by the pool should tend to offset one another, to a great extent.

Measuring each participant's stake

The stake of each scheme that has entrusted cash to the managers of the fund is measured in units. At the outset each scheme is allocated a number of units that is in proportion to the cash the scheme has contributed to the fund.

The managers use the income that the securities generate, as dividends or interest, to buy additional securities. These increase the value of the fund and of its units.

When a scheme pays further money in, the managers buy additional securities, and the number of units the scheme holds increases. When a scheme draws money out to pay benefits, the number of units it holds decreases.

Keeping a float

That is the simplest way to view what happens. In practice the managers always hold part of the fund's assets in cash, so as to be able to meet the demands of schemes that need to sell units to pay benefits.

When a new scheme wishes to join the fund, the managers allot the number of units appropriate to the amount of cash paid into the fund, and the managers may take the opportunity to widen the spread of securities even further.

Checking the effectiveness of a fund

Obviously it is impossible to guarantee that the value of units will never go down. Stock markets go through good and bad periods. If the variations in the value of the underlying investments of a fund match a yardstick such as the FT index, the fund is doing reasonably well.

The more highly developed managements operate various different kinds of fund. A life office may have a gilt-edged fund, an equity fund, a property fund and one or more mixed funds. The people responsible for a pension scheme may then need advice on how to allocate their cash to the various funds.

Taking care of mortality risks

There are at least two ways in which a pension scheme with a handful of members could suffer a severe loss because of the brevity or exceptional length of one member's life. If a member died soon after the scheme started, a cash sum greater than the amount in the fund might be payable. On the other hand if a pensioner lived for long enough to receive a telegram from the Queen, the scheme's fund might have been seriously depleted, many years earlier.

To guard against the possible effects of these risks, it is prudent for the scheme to insure against them with a life assurance company. A term assurance to provide the appropriate lump sum on the death of a member before pension age is fairly inexpensive. And the purchase price for an annuity for a retiring member will take account of the possibility that he or she may not live for many years, as well as the risk that annuity payments will have to be made for a very long time.

Making comprehensive provision

Actuaries and investment specialists play important parts in the organisation of life assurance companies. In the circumstances it is not surprising that many employers are happy to hand over the organising of their pension schemes to those life offices which have long experience of this work. They are skilled in arranging schemes for any number of employees, from one upwards.

Catering for individuals

A one-employee scheme has been referred to by such names as 'Top Hat' or 'Executive' at various times. That does not mean that it is suitable only for such exalted people. Self-employed professional people often employ full-time or part-time secretaries and make pension provision for them by means of policies that will also include protection for dependants of the employees.

The same kinds of policy may also be used for each member of a handful of employees of a single employer. It could be said that each policy is then a building block in the construction of the employer's pension scheme. It is, of course, a self-contained block. The benefits it provides relate solely to the employee for whom it was created. No other member of the scheme has any claim to any part of that block.

Handling medium-sized groups

Where an employer wants to install a pension scheme for, say, 20 or more members, it is usual to set up a group scheme in which the money for paying the retirement benefits, when they become due, is accumulated in a central fund. The amount of the fund may be expressed in money terms or as a number of units. The latter will apply if the life office operates a unit trust system.

The employer provides the life office with details of the members of the scheme, including their dates of birth, length of service and earnings, and agrees the basis of the scheme with the life office. The office provides a draft of possible rules for the scheme and invites the employer to discuss it with the employer's legal adviser.

When rules for the scheme have been agreed and adopted, the life office usually submits the scheme to the relevant authorities for their approval – see Chapter 6 – and provides booklets describing the scheme, for the employer to distribute among the members (see Figure 3).

However, where a scheme has only one member, it is a common practice to simplify the paperwork. In place of a booklet plus a note giving formal confirmation of membership, the employee receives a letter from the employer. This says that the employer is setting up a pension arrangement for the employee, under trust, names the trustee(s) and gives all the significant details of the employee's entitlements and duties under the arrangement. The employee signs a copy of the letter, acknowledging that he has received it and agrees to the terms. This procedure is usually referred to as 'establishing a pension arrangement by an exchange of letters'.

Appointing trustees

Since 1997 the law has required that at least a third of the trustees of a pension scheme must be appointed by the members. Also at least

---

Introduction

Identity and duties of trustees

Who pays the cost

Normal pension date

Basis of pension

Options at retirement

Early or late retirement

Leaving service of employer

Death in service benefits

Death in retirement benefits

If you have any questions

Fig. 3. Contents of scheme members' booklets.

two of the trustees must be appointed by the members *unless there are fewer than 100 members*. In that case, one will suffice. The employer may appoint the others.

This insistence on member-appointed trustees may appear to imply that those trustees are there for the specific purpose of looking after the interests of the members. In fact it is a duty of all trustees to act in the interests of all the beneficiaries of the trust of which they are trustees. This was a principle of trust law before pension schemes were thought of.

Note, too, the reference to 'all the *beneficiaries*'. Each trustee of a pension scheme has equal duties to look after the interests of widows and other dependants of a member who have rights under the rules of the scheme, and to look after the interests of the members themselves. Also included within the description of 'beneficiaries' are:

- retired employees who are already drawing pensions, and

- former employees who have frozen rights in the scheme and will be entitled to draw pensions from the scheme, in due course.

Recognising trustee duties

It is essential that all the people who are concerned with the management of a scheme appreciate that they must allow the trustees to do their job. To this end, it is desirable that all new trustees should receive professional training for their role.

Among the specific duties of trustees of a pension scheme are:

- investing the fund in appropriate securities, after taking account of reliable professional advice

- achieving appropriate diversification of investments

- checking, at appropriate intervals, the continued appropriateness of existing investments

- receiving regular actuarial advice on the adequacy of the funding of the scheme and recommendations regarding future contributions

- checking that any contributions deducted from members' pay and all contributions due from the employer have been duly invested

- exercising any discretion given by the scheme rules regarding the destination of any lump sum payable on the death of a member.

INVESTING THE CONTRIBUTIONS FOR PERSONAL PENSIONS

The general limitation on personal pensions, as applied to self-employed people, is that their contributions in a year must not exceed a given percentage of their 'net relevant earnings'. The percentage depends on the contributor's age on 6 April at the beginning of the tax year for which the contribution is made. **Relevant earnings** are effectively earnings that are not pensionable by any other arrangement.

Example
If Bill's only earnings are his salary from an employer to whose pension scheme Bill belongs, he has no *relevant earnings*.

On the other hand, Leslie, who is in the same employment and scheme as Bill, earns not only his salary from that employment but also fees as a freelance musician in his spare time. Those fees are *relevant earnings*. Leslie's *net relevant earnings* are his fees minus any expenses that he incurs to earn his fees and that are allowed as a deduction from his fees, for tax purposes.

There is an upper limit to the earnings that can be taken into account as net relevant earnings. For the tax year 1998/9 it is £87,600. The limit is normally increased, each year, in line with the Retail Prices Index. The maximum percentages of net relevant earnings that can be paid into a personal pension are shown in Figure 4.

Looking at old style plans
Personal pensions, as they have been described up to this point, began on 1 July 1988. Before that date the corresponding plans were often referred to as 'retirement annuities'. That was the label attached in the 1956 Finance Act, which was the legislation that introduced the tax advantages the annuities offered. People who still have such arrangements may continue to contribute to them. They may also increase their contributions to them, up to the less generous limits that apply to them, as shown in Figure 4. But they are not subject to the earnings limit (or 'cap') to which the previous paragraph refers. Because of this, some high earners may be wise to give no second thought to the attractive higher percentage contributions permitted for post-1988 personal pensions. A lower percentage of

Pre July 1988 Cases

Age	% net relevant earnings
up to 50	17.5
51–55	20
56–60	22.5
61–74	27.5

Post July 1988 Cases

Age	% net relevant earnings*
16–35	17.5
36–45	20
46–50	25
51–55	30
56–60	35
61–74	40

*subject to upper earnings limit

Fig. 4. Maximum annual contributions to Personal Pension as percentage of net relevant earnings.

larger earnings may be greater than the higher percentage of 'capped' earnings.

Comparing available investments

A requirement for old style personal pensions was that they were arranged 'with a person lawfully carrying on in the United Kingdom the business of granting annuities on human life'. This effectively limited the choice to life assurance companies and friendly societies.

Over the years such companies and societies have greatly increased the range of choices they offer for selecting how contributions should be invested, in the hope of maximising the retirement benefits. The traditional life office choice of without profit or with profit was easy to make. In 99 per cent of the time the with profit policy achieved the better result. When unit trusts, with a range of types of investment to choose from, were on offer, how should a lay person choose?

Add the facility to switch between funds, as the spirit moved one, and obtaining the best result could be as difficult as winning the National Lottery. In the circumstances, Chapter 12 (on independent advice) is the most important chapter in this book for many readers.

For the moment, suffice it to point out that:

- bonus additions to traditional with profit benefits cannot be taken away once they have been added

- a facility to switch one's accumulating holdings between funds has been dubbed 'a facility for always switching in the wrong direction at the wrong time'.

You need to look further than that comparison before deciding where to invest your personal pension contributions.

POINTS TO CONSIDER

1. Bearing in mind the progressive increase in the proportion of the population that will be retired during the next century, have you started planning how to maintain your standard of living?

2. If you have, will you be keeping a note of any clues you find, in this book or elsewhere?

3 Do you think it should be compulsory for the trustees of a pension scheme to include at least one member who is already retired and drawing a pension from the scheme?

5
Looking at Taxation

'The avoidance of taxes is the only pursuit that still carries any reward.' Those words are attributed to John Maynard Keynes, a respected economist of the *first* half of the 20th century. He recognised the essential difference between tax *avoidance* and tax *evasion*. He would have appreciated some of the tax reliefs that UK pensions arrangements have enjoyed in the *second* half of the century.

TAXING STATE PENSIONS

You already know, from Chapter 4, that the NI contributions you make, either as an employee or as an employer – or even as both – go into an enormous fund. It finances government expenditure. That includes the cost of paying state pensions.

But what is the status of those pensions, in relation to the dealings of the recipients with the Inland Revenue? The personal allowance, for income tax purposes, is usually approximately equal to the basic state pension. So the payment of that pension may appear to be free of tax, at first sight. However, if you were already receiving an income from other sources, before payment of your state pension started, the Inland Revenue would take steps to collect income tax on your additional income – in other words, on your state pension. In the final analysis, the sequence in which your sources of taxable income become part of your financial support system is of little account. Eventually they add up to the same total.

Quoting your number
In this context, it may not have occurred to you that the Inland Revenue and the Department of Social Security have one important thing in common, concerning your state pension. They share the same reference number for your financial affairs. So when you come to start drawing your state pension, the Inland Revenue will know its amount as soon as you will.

CONTRIBUTING TO OCCUPATIONAL PENSIONS

The primary source of a pension fund is the contributions it receives to enable the managers of the fund to pay pensions when they become due. The essential contributor to the fund is the employer. If the scheme obtains approval by the Inland Revenue (see Chapter 6) the employer can claim those contributions as business expenditure, for tax purposes.

The members of the scheme may be required to contribute to the fund, too, as one of the conditions of membership. If the scheme is established under trust and granted exempt approval by the Inland Revenue, those contributions will be treated as an allowable expense, for tax purposes. They will be deducted from the members' earnings before their income tax liability is calculated by the PAYE system. This ensures that they receive tax relief on their contributions.

Additional voluntary contributions

Whether the rules of a scheme require members to contribute to the fund or not, any member may make voluntary contributions to increase the benefits payable for him or her. The employer must permit this, as long as those contributions would not increase benefits beyond limits imposed by the law. Such contributions are known as additional voluntary contributions (AVCs). They are additional to the contributions the rules require the employer to make, and to any they require the member to make.

Financing supplementary benefits

Note that the object is to increase the benefits *for* the member. Think of a member who has a severely handicapped child. Arranging for the scheme to pay a pension for the child, in addition to a pension for the member's widow(er), after the member's death, could be a great boon for the family.

If you would like to increase the benefits your employer's scheme provides for you and your dependants by making AVCs, ask what facilities are available under the scheme. It may offer a choice of pension providers. Whether they are few or many, examine and compare each of them carefully. Compare them also with the terms offered by other possible pension providers. (Most of these are life assurance companies.)

Compare the track records of the providers. How effectively have they invested contributions entrusted to them in the past? It may not be an infallible guide to their future performance, but a provider that regularly appears in the top 25 per cent in the tables published by the financial press is likely to achieve better results than one that rarely lifts itself out of the bottom 25 per cent.

Checking out the pension providers

Compare any charges the providers make for the service they provide. They may be substantial. It is better to know all about them before committing yourself to a regime. You may discover that one or more of the providers the trustees of your scheme use will waive charges when dealing with AVCs for members of the scheme. Such a detail, although helpful, should not necessarily outweigh other considerations, but it deserves careful thought.

Your researches may convince you that one of the providers that is not connected with the scheme offers the best prospects. If that is so, you can choose to make your AVCs to that provider. You will then be making what are known as free-standing AVCs (FSAVCs). Many people do this, with excellent results. But if the amount of your intended AVC is substantial, you might be wise to seek independent advice – see Chapter 12.

Receiving income tax relief

The way in which you receive income tax relief on your AVCs will depend on whether the provider you choose is one used by the scheme or not. If it is a provider on the scheme's list, your AVCs will be deducted from your pay in the same way as any compulsory contribution, and your employer's PAYE return will show your net pay, after the deduction.

If you choose a pension provider that is not on the scheme's list, you will pay your FSAVCs direct to the provider, *after deducting income tax at the standard rate from the amount of each payment.* The provider will reclaim the income tax from the Inland Revenue, and you will be in the same position, in relation to income tax, as you would have been in if the FSAVCs had been deducted from your pay.

PAYING FOR PERSONAL PENSIONS

Some people spend their lives regretting missed opportunities. In the world of personal pensions, there is more time than usual to seize them. The late payment of a contribution may not invalidate it for purposes of income tax relief.

When making a contribution to a personal pension, you can also make a contribution in respect of any of the preceding six tax years for which you have not made the maximum qualifying contribution.

If you are not in a position to pay the whole amount, three rules will apply:

1. You must **not** have been a member of an occupational pension scheme during the relevant years.

2. You must make the maximum contribution for the current tax year.

3. You must apply the balance of what you pay, firstly to the earliest of those years, and then to the others, in sequence.

The example in Figure 5 illustrates how this facility may operate.

Roger is a self-employed businessman who started a personal pension, ten years ago. The following table shows the maximum contributions his earnings justified and the actual contributions he made, since he started.

Year	Maximum	Actual	Unused
1	£3,000	£3,000	
2	3,100	3,000	£100
3	2,900	2,000	900
4	2,500	1,800	700
5	2,000	nil	2,000
6	1,500	nil	1,500
7	1,550	nil	1,550
8	1,700	nil	1,700
9	2,400	nil	2,400
10	3,900		

If Roger can now afford to pay £7,000, this will absorb £3,900 relief for the current tax year, £700 for year 4, £2,000 for year 5, and £400 of the unused relief for year 6 (leaving £1,100 relief for that year still unused).

Fig. 5. Example of how the holder of a personal pension may use earlier tax years' unused tax relief.

Picking up earlier opportunities

There is an additional situation which sometimes offers scope for making a larger contribution. Tax assessments for self-employed people may take a long time to agree with the Inland Revenue. Where they do not become 'final and conclusive' until more than six years have elapsed since the end of the year to which they relate, all is not lost. Within six months of an assessment's becoming final and conclusive, the taxpayer may make a contribution in respect of the net relevant earnings in that earlier tax year and elect that relief is given in the year in which the contribution is actually made.

Another aspect of contributing to a personal pension that deserves mention is that there are occasions when a shortage of current income ought not to hinder making a contribution. If there is an accumulation of unused tax relief, providing the necessary cash by drawing savings out of a building society can be profitable. This is particularly true when you are nearing the age at which you intend to stop paying for a pension and start drawing it.

Receiving tax relief on personal pension contributions

To avoid any possible confusion, it may be as well to point out that income tax relief on personal pension contributions is given by allowing them as deductions from income before assessing what tax is payable for the year that is under review. So a contribution may be made in connection with an earlier year. But any investment rewards, such as bonuses, relating to the contribution, will take effect from the date when the provider receives the contribution.

NOTING IMPORTANT TAXATION CHANGES

For 40 years or more, the principles concerning the taxation of pension fund investments were largely unchanged. The managers and trustees of funds relating to occupational pension schemes and personal pensions were able to reclaim tax credits on the income they had received from their investments.

On 2 July 1997, the Chancellor of the Exchequer announced that the reclaiming of such tax credits would cease immediately. He had been appointed in the aftermath of the General Election, two months earlier, and had the task of presenting a budget to finance the new government's programme.

His action dealt a severe blow to the contributors to all those funded pensions. Unless they could find the wherewithal to increase their contributions, the benefits that would be payable would be noticeably smaller than had been intended.

If you were already a member of a funded occupational scheme or were contributing to a personal pension, you would be well advised to find out how the Chancellor's announcement is affecting your pension prospects. Has anybody launched a damage-limitation exercise? Ought you to be taking the initiative yourself?

Limiting the damage

The trustees of an occupational scheme should appreciate the respective responsibilities of the various parties and how they differ between one type of scheme and another.

Deciding who pays

An important way of dividing schemes into two groups is to separate contributory schemes from non-contributory schemes. In the first group, a regular deduction – usually a fixed percentage – is made from each member's pay. The basis of the deduction is laid down in the rules of the scheme, probably with no provision for variation. So if any adjustment is to be made to contributions, to counteract the effect of the withdrawal of tax relief on investment income, it will have to be made entirely by the employer, unless the members agree to share the load.

Comparing two benefit bases

If the basis of a scheme is money purchase, the employer may reasonably decide that the rules impose no duty on anybody to try to lessen the impact of the tax change. After all, nobody would expect employers to increase wages so as to nullify the effect of an increase in the basic rate of income tax. However, it would be a helpful gesture, on the employer's part, to draw the attention of the members of the scheme to the effect of the Chancellor's action. And a reminder that individual members could make AVCs, to offset the loss of tax credits, might not come amiss.

In a final salary scheme, the position is different. The employer has an obligation to provide the defined benefits, come hell or high water. That imposes on the employer's actuarial adviser a duty to take the effect of the loss of the tax credit payments into account when assessing what contributions the employer should make, to ensure that the trustees will be able to meet their obligations.

Taking action yourself

Are you paying for a personal pension? If you are, you may have already realised that 2 July 1997 was a bad day for you. It was the day when the future build-up of your benefits took a cut.

What are you going to do about it? What *can* you do? If you are already making maximum permissible contributions, there is nothing else you can do. If you are contributing less than the maximum, you can increase your contributions as far as your purse and the legal limits permit.

- Are you a member of an occupational pension scheme that promises you smaller benefits than it could provide?

- If 'yes', what are you doing about it?

- For your dependants' sake, as well as your own, start paying AVCs.

CHECKLIST

- The Department of Social Security does **not** deduct income tax from your state pension, but **does** advise the Inland Revenue of the amount of that pension.

- If you also have an occupational pension, your PAYE coding will take account of your state pension.

- If you pay FSAVCs, you deduct income tax at the standard rate, before paying each contribution.

- If you have a personal pension, you may be able to make a contribution for earlier years in which you did not make the maximum qualifying contribution.

6
Satisfying the Relevant Authorities

Matthew Arnold, the poet and critic, referred to 'an Englishman's heaven-born privilege of doing as he likes'. That was more than 100 years ago, when relatively few people had a pension to look forward to. Nowadays it would be truer to say that privileges often impose restrictions. They certainly do in the world of pension schemes. They also offer opportunities.

Identifying the authorities

There are two bodies that have vital roles to play in relation to pension scheme duties. The Pension Schemes Office of the Inland Revenue has a duty to check that schemes comply with taxation requirements. The Occupational Pensions Regulatory Authority has responsibility for checking that the trustees of pension schemes are obeying the Pension Schemes Act 1993 and the Pensions Act 1995. These are designed to look after the interests of members. They relate not only to the appointment and conduct of trustees but also to the solvency of schemes. They also deal with using occupational schemes or personal pensions for contracting-out of SERPS. They are intended to ensure that your pension scheme provides benefits for you and your dependants as it should.

Sounding a cautionary note

It is important to bear in mind that the world of pensions is highly mobile. This chapter is being written in January 1998. Limitations imposed by the authorities that are mentioned above, or by Parliament, are quoted as they appear to be in that month. The benefits of many people who are now members of pension schemes are subject to limitations that do not apply to schemes that are being set up today but still apply to existing members of those schemes. Always remember that it is the rules of the scheme to which you belong that govern your benefits.

QUALIFYING FOR TAXATION ADVANTAGES

With hundreds of thousands of pension schemes to approve, the staff of the Pension Scheme Office (PSO) must satisfy themselves that the schemes are being set up in good faith. Their sole purpose must be to provide what the PSO defines as relevant benefits. Their Practice Notes emphasise this.

The Notes take up more than 150 sheets of A4 paper. That is far more paper than this book contains. They are for the guidance of the PSO's own staff and all the advisers, consultants and other people who draft documents for pension schemes. The objective is to achieve documentation that will justify the PSO's giving exempt approval to the schemes. That approval will enable the employers' contributions to be:

- treated as a business expense, for tax purposes, and
- **not** treated as taxable benefits of the members of the schemes.

Knowing who are employees

After stating the cardinal principle that a scheme must be established under irrevocable trusts, the Notes go on to make it clear that nobody who is not a genuine employee of the employer can be admitted to membership of a scheme. Sole proprietors and partners are not employees: they are principals.

Checking a director's status

Company directors are not necessarily excluded from membership. For example, a director of a public limited company who received fees for attending board meetings might be eligible for membership of the company's pension scheme. However, if she attended meetings in the capacity of a professional woman who was offering professional advice to the board, and she had to account for her fees to her partners in a professional practice, she would be ineligible for membership of the scheme.

Trustees need reliable advice before admitting a director to membership of their scheme.

Identifying permissible benefits

Having made those points, the Notes spell out what benefits may be provided and in what circumstances. Some of the formulae derive from long-standing practice. For example, the target of a retirement pension that is two-thirds of final earnings matches the pension that

Charles Lamb, the essayist, received when he retired from the East India Company in 1825.

Other features doubtless derived from the Civil Service's own staff pensions' practice, but the people responsible for the production of the Notes have not slavishly followed precedents. They have taken account of changes in the employment scene, and they continue to do so.

The PSO issues frequent updates to the Notes.

ADOPTING ACCEPTABLE RETIREMENT AGES

Chapter 2 mentioned that any retirement age between 50 and 75 was acceptable to the PSO, and that an age outside that range could be approved, if it was appropriate to a member's job.

It is necessary for the rules of a scheme to stipulate a normal retirement age. Without that fixed point, an actuary would be unable to check the solvency of the scheme's invested fund and the adequacy of the contributions being made to it.

Using discretion

It is permissible, at times, for a scheme to have a discretionary normal retirement age. This may be to permit different employees to have different retirement ages to take account of the nature of their work. For example, a test pilot probably retires earlier than the mechanics who service the aircraft he tests. Discretionary normal retirement ages may also be appropriate where an employer wishes to recuit employees with specialised skills, which are rare enough for their possessors to be able to negotiate their own terms of employment.

Wherever a scheme has discretionary normal retirement ages, the actuary must be given details of the members involved and their entitlements.

A different way of making provision for a few employees who want bespoke normal retirement ages is to set up individual pension arrangements for them. These resemble the provision that an independent consultant may make for a private secretary, as is mentioned in Chapter 4.

OBSERVING LIMITS TO NORMAL RETIREMENT PENSION

The PSO sets out limits by reference to 'final remuneration'. Each scheme's rules must define that expression within parameters that the

Practice Notes describe, with lengthy ifs and buts. In simpler terms, final remuneration should not exceed *either*:

- the highest remuneration for any one of the preceding five years *or*

- the yearly average of the total emoluments for any three or more consecutive years in the last ten.

For this purpose, both 'remuneration' and 'emoluments' refer to taxable earnings from the employment, and 'remuneration' means basic pay for that year plus the yearly average over that year and two or more immediately preceding consecutive years of any fluctuating earnings (such as overtime or commission). Where earlier years' earnings are taken into account, they may be revalued in line with the retail prices index.

Acknowledging complications

Even this simplified version of the criteria may be gobbledegook to you. If so, don't let it worry you. You have no need to understand it. It is included for the benefit of:

- those readers who always want to delve more deeply than others

- those whose work compels them to try to understand it.

The basic formula for calculating the maximum pension that a scheme may provide at normal retirement age is 1/60th of final remuneration for each year of service, up to a maximum of 40 years. This permits the two-thirds of pay that many people regard as the norm. But with 60 as the normal pension age, how many university graduates could qualify for a two-thirds pension by that formula?

Allowing for additional relevant factors

The situation of the late entrant into pensionable employment is the easiest to deal with. Practice Notes say that such a person may be given a pension of up to 1/30th of final remuneration for each year of service up to a maximum of 20 years. That comes back to the two-thirds pension.

Nowadays few people work for the same employer from when they leave full-time education until they retire. Some change their jobs to increase their incomes. Others move to achieve more congenial working conditions, or to fit in with domestic changes. Many find themselves redundant – possibly more than once. For all these reasons, and others, people's pension scheme experience varies greatly.

Having retained benefits

Wherever a change of employment leads to the provision of what the Notes refer to as 'retained benefits', the new employer must be told about them and take them into account. Chapter 7 gives examples of types of retained benefits.

How do these benefits affect the pension prospects of somebody who is starting a new job that is by no means his first? Usually the 30ths formula, mentioned above, will apply, as long as the pension on that basis, plus any retained benefits, does not exceed 2/3rds of final remuneration.

MAKING PROVISION FOR WIDOWS AND DEPENDANTS

Modern pension schemes usually provide some form of death benefit if a member dies while still in service. It may be an immediate cash sum only; it may be a pension for the member's widow or another dependant. Many schemes provide both.

Providing a lump sum

The Practice Note allows payment of a sum that does not exceed the greater of:

- £5,000

- four times the member's final remuneration minus any such benefit* deriving from a previous employment.

*This deduction is unlikely to be relevant unless the member has been and/or is a controlling director.

Figure 3 gives an example of how choosing a recipient for the lump sum may be made subject to the discretion of the trustees, and why.

Providing pensions for widows and other dependants

A scheme may provide a pension for the widow or widower of a member or for somebody who was financially dependent on a member. The amount of the pension must not exceed two-thirds of the maximum that could have been approved for the member if he or she had retired, on grounds of incapacity, on the day of his or her death. (See Chapter 9.)

A scheme may provide pensions for two or more such people. The aggregate of all such pensions must not exceed one and a half times the maximum amount for each of them. A pension for a child must cease when the child ceases to be a dependant. A pension for a widow or widower may cease on remarriage or cohabitation, but most employers would be reluctant to burden trustees with responsibility for policing such a provision.

Including benefits payable when a member dies in retirement

Generally schemes do not provide lump sums payable on a member's death in retirement. There is one exception. Many schemes include a provision that a member's pension will continue to be payable for at least five years from the date of retirement even if the member dies. Often the scheme rules say that the remaining instalments for that guaranteed period will be payable as a lump sum. The rules may also give the trustees the same discretion regarding the choice of payee as those for lump sums payable on death in service.

Schemes usually also provide a pension for a widow, widower or dependant payable on the death of the member in retirement. The maximum amount of such a pension is two-thirds of the maximum pension the member could have received at retirement. The maximum aggregate of two or more pensions for people in those categories is one and a half times the maximum for one of them.

The comments made earlier about child dependants and widows who remarry or cohabit also apply here.

Permitting retiring members to allocate part of their pensions

Before starting to receive his or her pension, a member may allocate part of that pension to provide a pension for the member's spouse or a dependant to begin after the member's death in retirement. It is immaterial whether or not the scheme is already providing a pension, payable after the member's death, to the object of the member's bounty.

The member may even allocate part of his or her post-retirement pension to provide pensions to commence after the member's death in retirement, for two or more beneficiaries, as long as the aggregate of those pensions does not exceed the member's residual pension.

RESTRICTING COMMUTATION OF PENSION FOR CASH

One of the most highly rated features of pension schemes is the option for a member who is about to retire to receive a lump sum in place of part of the pension. This is referred to as 'commuting part of the pension for cash'. The option appeals to people for at least two major reasons.

The first reason is that, whereas the pension is taxable as income, the lump sum is not taxable. The second reason is that the lump sum is often of the order of one and a half years' pay. Many people have never before had so much ready money at their disposal before.

 Deciding how much cash is available
It is only to be expected that there will be strict limits imposed on how much of one's pension one can commute for a tax-free sum. A Practice Note says 'The maximum lump sum benefit payable, without taking account of the level of total benefits being provided for the employee, is 3/80ths of final remuneration for each year of service up to 40 years'.

Commuting trivial pensions
There must be justification for deciding that it would be unreasonable to insist that the trustees of a scheme must pay a member's benefit at retirement in the form of a pension, *however trivial the amount of the instalments would be*. The PSO agrees.

The extent of the agreement may surprise you. If the total amounts of all the benefits payable to a member under schemes related to the employment do not exceed £260 per annum, they may be commuted.

Including widows', widowers' and dependants' pensions
The principle that justifies commuting members' trivial pensions is equally valid for applying the facility to pensions for widows, widowers and dependants of members. The Practice Notes permit it. They go a step further. They allow it not only when those pensions become payable but also if and when the member commutes his own pension on grounds of triviality.

Retiring in serious ill-health
If a member retires 'in exceptional circumstances of serious ill-health' he or she may be permitted to commute the whole of his or her own pension (except *guaranteed minimum pension* or protected rights – relating to being contracted out). The PSO insists that adequate med-

ical evidence must be obtained by the trustees, satisfying them that the member's 'expectation of life is unquestionably very short, *ie* less than one year'.

Noting tax treatment
It is important to know that lump sums payable in some of these cases do not escape tax liability.

No tax liability arises in respect of widows', widowers' or dependants' pensions that have been commuted on grounds of triviality.

But commutation of a member's pension on grounds of triviality may give rise to tax charges against the scheme. The rules of the scheme may give power to deduct any such charges from the commutation payment.

Full commutation of a member's pension on the grounds of exceptional circumstances of serious ill-health gives rise to a charge to tax.

Where tax is charged in any of these circumstances, the rate of tax is 20 per cent.

COMPLYING WITH LIMITATIONS TO CONTRIBUTIONS

One of the conditions of approval of a scheme, other than an FSAVC scheme, is that the employer must contribute to the cost. A mere token contribution is not enough. Contributing less than 10 per cent would be inadequate. And where a scheme is effectively a collection of individual arrangements, the employer is expected to contribute at least 10 per cent of the cost of each of them.

Looking at members' contributions
A member's contributions may fall into any of three categories:

1. Compulsory contributions, required by the scheme rules.
2. Additional voluntary contributions (AVCs) made to the scheme.
3. Free-standing AVCs (FSAVCs) made to an FSAVC scheme.

The maximum aggregate contribution under the three headings must not exceed 15 per cent of the member's remuneration from the employment for which retirement benefits are being provided.

The member qualifies for tax relief on his contributions. For the first two categories, relief comes through the employer's pay system, by deducting the contributions from his or her pay before calculating the PAYE tax liability. For FSAVCs the member deducts tax from each contribution before remitting it to the FSAVC scheme.

MAKING A SALARY SACRIFICE

When is a contribution not a contribution? When it's a salary sacrifice. The idea may well have originated in the days before personal pensions began. An employee who had a good salary but no pension provision wanted to repair the omission. His employer was unwilling to make the necessary contribution. He was already paying the man handsomely. So the employee said he would forgo part of his salary if the employer would use the amount forgone as a contribution to a one-man pension scheme. The employer had nothing to lose, and agreed and set up the scheme.

A salary sacrifice appealed also to somebody whose employer was already contributing adequately but who wanted to contribute more than the maximum 15 per cent of his remuneration. Although the sacrifice would reduce the final remuneration on which the limits to his benefits would depend, he was confident that the overall effect would be to his advantage.

Satisfying the PSO

The PSO's predecessors soon cottoned on to what was happening and saw no need to reject the ploy totally. A Practice Note now spells out how to document such an arrangement. It also requires the employer to notify the appropriate Schedule E District, if the sacrifice is £5,000 or more per annum. The appropriate Schedule E District is the tax office that deals with the Income Tax payments under PAYE for the employer's employees.

QUALIFYING FOR CONTRACTING OUT OF SERPS

The state earnings related pension scheme (SERPS) is intended to ensure that every member of it qualifies for an additional pension to supplement the basic state pension. Many people are in occupational schemes that are likely to provide greater benefits than SERPS. Many others pay for personal pensions that are virtually certain to outperform SERPS. In either of these circumstances it is not surprising that people may want to contract-out of SERPS.

Seeing what SERPS costs and what it provides

Before taking the plunge, if you are at present in SERPS, you need to look at the scene so far. Chapter 1 mentioned that there are lower and upper earnings limits for National Insurance contributions. Employees who earn less than the lower limit pay nothing. Those who earn between the lower and upper limits contribute at a low rate on earnings up to the lower limit, and a higher rate on earnings between the lower and upper limits.

A SERPS pension is based on the pensioner's earnings between those limits – referred to as **middle band earnings** – in the tax years during which he or she contributed. Each year's such earnings are revalued in line with national average earnings, to allow for inflation.

For someone who reaches state pension age before 6 April 1999, the SERPS pension will be 1.25 per cent of revalued middle band earnings for each tax year between 6 April 1978 and state pension age. If there are more than 20 years of such revalued earnings, the best 20 will be used. In other words, the maximum SERPS pension will be 25 per cent of the average of the best 20 years' middle band earnings.

Changing benefits from 1999

For anyone who reaches state pension age after 5 April 1999, the SERPS pension will be a percentage of the average revalued middle band earnings throughout his or her membership of SERPS. The percentage will reduce from 25 per cent to 20 per cent by one half of one per cent, each year, starting on 6 April 2000.

Considering alternatives to SERPS

That reduction of the value of future SERPS pensions may encourage some contracting out. Other changes might influence people in the opposite direction. It is not possible to say with certainty whether being in SERPS or contracting out will produce the best retirement package of benefits, at the end of the road. So many factors might change. The heart of the problem is that successive Chancellors of the Exchequer have to deal with the financing of such diverse 'flavours of the month' in the priorities of government thinking.

Contracting out

There are two routes to contracting out:

- joining an occupational pension scheme that is contracted out
- taking out an appropriate personal pension.

When SERPS started on 6 April 1978, occupational pension schemes that provided benefits on an acceptable final remuneration basis were able to contract out the members after making minor adjustments to the rules. Ten years later it became possible to contract out members of money purchase schemes.

The objective must be to provide for each member a retirement pension and a widow's pension, both on death in service and on death in retirement, that is no less than SERPS would have provided. Most contracted out schemes achieve all these with a margin, in spite of the requirements having been simplified since SERPS started.

Using an appropriate personal pension

How can a personal pension, designed to enable self-employed people to provide pensions for their own retirement, be relevant to contracting out of SERPS? Surely SERPS relates only to employees!

That is true. It is also the reason for including the word 'appropriate'. An employee who either:

- is in an employment that has no pension scheme, or
- is in a pension scheme that is not contracted out

can have an appropriate personal pension. The employee and the pension provider complete form APP1 jointly and send it to the DSS, who send the rebate from the employee's and employer's NI contributions to the provider after the end of each tax year.

The provider puts the rebates into a separate fund from the other contributions to the appropriate personal pension. They constitute protected rights, available only in pension form from state pension age.

CHECKLIST

- The Pensions Schemes Office (PSO) and the Occupational Pensions Regulatory Authority (OPRA) have complementary roles, aimed at seeing schemes deal fairly and safely with members' benefits.

- Practice Notes are designed to permit retirement at a time compatible with occupation, health and current employment practice.

- Primarily a scheme should provide a pension for each member, but lump sums may be allowed to:
  - comply with pension scheme tradition
  - avoid the need to pay trivial amounts in the form of pensions
  - help a member whose death from illness is almost imminent.

- A scheme may provide pensions for dependants, payable after a member's death, whether while in service or in retirement.

- Contributions should be adequate to pay for the benefits, but not excessive.

- A range of choices is available for dealing with benefits of a member whose employment changes.

- A suitable scheme or appropriate personal pension may be used to contract out of SERPS.

7
Changing Your Job

They say that a change is as good as a rest, but there is usually nothing restful about changing one's job. It is more likely to be stressful, at least initially.

HAVING THE URGE

This chapter is primarily concerned with an occasion when you want to move to another employment. You may want to widen your experience or to have a more responsible position. You may want to spend less time in travelling to and from your work or to have a pleasanter environment. You may even have taken a few years out of employment, for family reasons, and believe that you could now do a more demanding job than the one you left.

Taking the initiative
Let there be no doubt in your mind, *you are taking the initiative*. The idea of seeking the job is yours. Somebody else may have put an advertisement wherever you saw it, but it was you who decided to apply for the job.

As you are taking the initiative, you want to make sure that all the terms of the job on offer are satisfactory. You may even be able to make suggestions about improving them. You might sense that the person interviewing you would appreciate constructive suggestions, if you made them tactfully, and take you on because of your making them.

Doing your homework in advance
You know what you have in mind. You have probably been thinking about it for weeks or more. You have a clear idea in your head, but have you listed all the features you are looking for, on paper. Arming yourself with such an *aide-memoire* could boost your morale and increase your self-confidence, as you approach an interview.

Familiarise yourself with all the details of your present employer's pension scheme before you are even offered an interview.

Being discreet

You will, of course, avoid acting in such a way as to give your superiors a clue to your intentions. It would be a pity if the person in charge of your employer's pension scheme happened to remark that you were taking a great interest in the Leaving Service Rule. You might detect a sudden cooling of the senior management's attitude towards you. They might take your name off a confidential list of candidates for promotion that they were preparing. (You would, of course, probably be unaware of this.)

Finding your scheme guide

What happened to the copy of the guide to the pension scheme that you were given when you joined it? The guide should tell you what happens about your benefits if you move to another job. It would pay you to find it, before you go any further. This chapter will supplement what the guide says.

Although all this information will not be uppermost in your mind during an interview, it could be helpful for you to be able to respond knowledgeably if the subject cropped up. Knowing that there is no sure-fire way to deal with one's accrued pension rights is important. What choices are there?

HAVING BENEFITS PRESERVED IN YOUR PRESENT EMPLOYER'S SCHEME

You may have equally valid reasons for leaving your accrued rights in your old employer's pension scheme and for moving them elsewhere, if you change your job. They deserve careful thought.

Contrasting circumstances

Situations sometimes develop where it would be embarrassing for an ex-employee to remain a member of the scheme. That must be a matter of judgement. You must pick up the vibes, if there are any.

There may be circumstances where it is a good idea to remain a member of your old employer's scheme. There is an old saying, 'The devil you know is better than the devil you don't'. If you have been with your present employer for several years, you might prefer that the retirement benefits that have built up, during that time, should stay where they are. You know and trust this employer, in spite of the fact that you are moving on.

(A generous employer might subsidise benefits for a respected former employee, so that they exceeded what the law required to be paid.)

If you change your mind, later, you can ask to have the value of the benefits transferred. Meanwhile, they will increase each year until your normal retirement date. The annual addition will be *not less than the smaller of*:

- the increase in the retail prices index and
- five per cent.

HAVING A TRANSFER PAYMENT MADE

You cannot have such a payment made to your current or deposit account with a bank or building society. It can only be made to one of three types of destination. They are:

- another occupational pension scheme
- an appropriate personal pension
- a section 32 buy-out policy.

Retirement benefits relating to the time you spend in your new employment must obviously be provided by a scheme relating to that employment. Your old employer's scheme does not do that.

There is no obligation for you to do anything in a hurry. You will doubtless be invited to join a scheme of your new employer, if there is one, but you may be on probation for a period of up to six months. That will give both you and the new employer time to decide whether either offering or accepting the job was a mistake. It will also give you time to ask the trustees of your present scheme to let you have a quotation of a transfer value in respect of your existing scheme benefits.

Noting different viewpoints

There is no unique figure for a transfer value. Opinions differ. They depend on whether one is buying or selling.

The Institute of Actuaries – which is one of the two bodies that control the professional qualification of actuaries – has issued a Guidance Note regarding the calculation of transfer values. However, there is inevitably an element of professional judgement involved.

Comparing professional advice

The actuary who advises the scheme that has to make a transfer payment needs to ensure that the scheme's fund is not weakened by making the payment. It would be wrong to let a departing member take more than a fair share of the fund.

A receiving scheme's actuary would be concerned to ensure that the scheme could afford to provide the benefits that are being recommended, in response to receiving the payment. He or she may suggest that more modest benefits should be provided. The onus will then be on the member to decide whether to have a transfer payment made on those terms or whether to seek a more attractive arrangement.

A Case study

Richard has been a member of a final salary pension scheme for eight years when he applies for, and is offered, a job with another employer. He accepts the job and starts to draw a salary 20 per cent greater than he had been receiving. He asks his previous employer for a quotation for a transfer value of his pension scheme benefits.

The bases of the old and new schemes are virtually identical. Each provides a pension at age 60 that is one sixtieth of final remuneration for each year of service. So Richard is disgusted when the new scheme's actuary tells him that the transfer value that has been offered will buy only three extra years' pension in the new scheme.

'It was meant to represent eight years' membership of the previous scheme,' he complained.

'I know that,' the actuary replied, 'But during most of those years you were earning far less than when you left that job. Not only that, but also the contributions that were made for you, in those years, would be invested to earn interest for more years before your 60th birthday than this company's contributions will be invested. In layman's language, those are just two of the things an actuary has to take into consideration. There are others, but I won't confuse you by trying to explain them to you.'

Richard was not convinced, but he had two more strings to his bow. He decided to try them, before making up his mind what to do.

Consulting alternatives

Both of the possibilities involved seeking quotations from other kinds of pension providers. First he asked for figures for a section 32 buyout policy from three life assurance companies that would accept payment of the transfer value and issue a with-profit policy to provide him with a pension at retirement. They confirmed that no other payments than the transfer value could be made to such a ↓

They also pointed out that the amount available to pay foɩ ⌐ pension, when he wanted to retire, would depend on the profits that had
been added to the policy between when they received the transfer
payment and when Richard retired. How much would be added
would depend on how much the companies earned by investing the
transfer value.

Trying another avenue
Richard's second possible choice was an appropriate personal pension. He invited quotations from three different kinds of pension
provider – a life assurance company, a friendly society and a unit trust
group.

Each of them quoted and also mentioned that an appropriate personal pension could accept not only a transfer value but also contributions from an employee whose employer had no pension scheme.
Suddenly the penny dropped. He had overlooked one important factor, when comparing what he was offered in exchange for a transfer
payment with what he gave up to obtain the payment. The actuaries
who calculated the payment, and the other people who quoted for
alternative pension provision, all had to be paid. The work of switching the source of his pension cost money. Unless somebody else was
willing to pay, the bill came to him.

None of the choices filled Richard with enthusiasm. For some days,
he debated whether to accept a transfer to his new employer's scheme
or leave the money where it was.

Achieving a happier solution
There is one factor that sometimes makes a great difference to the
situation. If an employer wants to recruit somebody who appears to
be the ideal candidate for the job, irksome snags may disappear. A
difference of opinion about what pension rights should be given may
vanish.

Providing a star recruit with the largest benefits the Practice Notes
will permit could be a worthwhile price to pay for engaging the right
person. Advising you on how to groom yourself to justify such VIP
treatment is beyond the scope of this book.

Maybe Richard discovered the recipe.

BRINGING SERPS INTO THE PICTURE

As long as you remain with the same employer, you can forget about SERPS. Either you are contracted out or you aren't. You know which, from having done your homework.

If you are contracted out under your present employer's scheme, part of the benefits that have accrued to you under the scheme are **protected rights**. They can only be paid to you in the form of a pension from state pension age. **This fact must be mentioned** to any pension provider to whom a transfer payment that includes their value is made.

The moment you have an offer of another job, the subject of SERPS crops up. You need to find out whether the prospective employer's scheme is contracted out or not.

If you are not contracted out at present and neither is the other scheme, there is nothing to alter. You will still be contributing to SERPS if you accept the job offer.

If you are not contracted out at present but the other scheme *is* contracted out, there is no problem. The person in charge of your new employer's PAYE system will ensure that your income tax and *reduced* NI contributions go through the correct channels.

If you *are* contracted out at present and so is the other scheme, there is no problem. This is the commonest situation, on a change of employment.

If you are contracted out at present, but the other scheme is not, you could remain contracted out, if you so wished, by using an appropriate personal pension and having the DSS rebate credited to it. Seeking independent advice as recommended by Chapter 12, might help you.

CHECKLIST

- Make a list of:
  - why you want the change
  - what you are looking for
  - what you have to offer a prospective employer
  - your rights under your pension scheme.

- When you have a satisfactory offer of a job:
  - accept it
  - give required notice to your present employer
  - obtain quotation of transfer value for your pension rights
  - ask your new employer for terms of entry to his scheme
  - decide whether to accept them or seek other alternatives
  - make final decision before transfer value quotation expires.

8
Suffering Amalgamation, Takeover or Hiving Off

It is part of the modern scene for companies to join with other companies, to form industrial giants, or to hive off parts of conglomerates as smaller, self-contained companies. For example, Brown & Co Plc approaches Green Plc and suggests that they might pursue their mutual interests in a joint venture, called 'Brogren Plc', instead of competing with each other.

A few years later, Brogren Plc sells all its freight transport facilities to Brentrans Plc. This is a new company that immediately provides freight transport services to Brogren Plc.

Within a few weeks, Brentrans Plc has expanded its garage and workshop area and signed contracts for freighting the goods of several other companies.

Doubtless the board of Brogren Plc are already formulating plans for their next reconstruction.

During the last 25 years, the process of creating commercial giants has been advanced in many areas, but most noticeably in the financial world of banks and building societies.

LOOKING AT THE PHENOMENON MORE CLOSELY

Sometimes the giants have taken over the pygmies. Sometimes they have merged their operations with those of similarly sized rivals. Recently some of the larger building societies have added banking to their other activities. And some building societies and insurance companies have bought up estate agencies. Some have apparently prospered. Others soon sold off the estate agencies that they had bought earlier.

The heading to this chapter relates to the situation of thousands of people in these industries, and in many others. How do their retirement prospects fare as a consequence of these reshuffles?

There is a comment about optimists and pessimists that may help you to take a positive view of this state of affairs:

A pessimist sees a difficulty in every opportunity.
An optimist sees an opportunity in every difficulty.

Keep your eyes open: see the opportunities in all these comings and goings, and seize them. That will be part of your preparing successfully for retirement.

POOLING RESOURCES AND LIABILITIES

When two companies amalgamate, they may well have broadly similar pension schemes that have investment portfolios with similar spreads of shareholdings. This should facilitate the merging of the funds, if this is agreed.

But reorganisation of the schemes needs more than approval by the boards and shareholders of the companies and by the trustees of the schemes. The Pension Schemes Office (PSO) need to be consulted. Without their approval, the changes cannot be put into force.

Checking on the finances

The granting of the PSO's approval is no mere formality. They may require actuarial reports on the assets and liabilities of the funds, and the proposed treatment of any surpluses that may be disclosed.

The purpose of checking on any apparent gain or loss to any scheme or employer, as a consequence of the proposed pension scheme changes, is not hard to find. The PSO is, of course, part of the Inland Revenue. Tax relief has been allowed in respect of the contributions that have been made to the funds, so tax is likely to be charged on a refund of any surplus.

AGGREGATING PENSIONABLE SERVICE

Juggling with the structure of a company and rearranging pension schemes is not everybody's cup of tea. Most of the employees have no wish to try to follow it in detail. What they want to know is, 'Shall I still get the same rate of pay and the same amount of pension, and other benefits, as I should have had, before all these changes happened?'

The PSO need to look at the restructuring more closely than that. They ask for information about the number of years' service that members who are being transferred to a new or different scheme will be credited with. If they are being given full credit, is there justification for saying that they are effectively still in the same employment as before the change?

Checking continuity of occupation
There is a traditional way of rephrasing that question. 'Is John Smith still sitting at the same desk and doing the same job?' (See Figure 6.)

That is fine, if John works for a bank or building society. What about if he drives a delivery van or digs holes in the road? Perhaps 'driving from the same garage' or 'based at the same depot' might fill the bill.

ADJUSTING CONTRIBUTIONS AND/OR BENEFITS

When one company takes over another, the pension rights of the

Fig. 6. Sitting at the same desk and doing the same job.

No, this isn't quite what the words in the heading are intended to mean. They relate to somebody whose employer has sold the business as a going concern, and who, for practical purposes, is unaffected by the change. In the circumstances, the PSO are happy to treat his employment as being continuous, when deciding what pension scheme benefits he can have.

employees of the company being taken over may differ from those of the other company's employees. There is no obvious reason why this should not be so.

What happens next is likely to depend on the reason for the takeover. If the buyer was keen to add an efficient complementary enterprise to an existing successful business, the transferring employees can breathe again. It is unlikely that they are destined for the discard. Their skill and experience is part of the valuable entity that inspired the takeover bid. They will clearly merit retirement benefits at least as good as those of the other company's employees.

Integrating the terms

To achieve ease of administration, the new company will want the basis of any contributions the members have to make to the pension scheme to be the same for old and new employees. If there is a historical difference between the terms, this will need to be ironed out by negotiation. The trustees of the scheme for the employees who have been taken over should be ideally situated to represent its members. They are well steeped in the structure of the scheme.

Their knowledge should also be helpful in ensuring that justice is done to any of those members who have been making AVCs to the scheme.

Looking ahead

As you read this, do you recognise the situation as one you are in? If so, you need to look ahead carefully. Economies of staff may – indeed probably will – come later. You need to leave the new management in no doubt that you are now an essential part of the amalgamated workforce. Quietly, but effectively, you must start selling that message as soon as the new management start work. You must plant it in their minds before the word 'economy' arrives. You must also be alert to note any clue to their intentions and be quick to fit yourself to take advantage of any opportunities that arise.

Considering a different scenario

Perhaps the purchasers of the company you were employed by viewed it as a moribund business – 'with possibilities'. They may have planned to engage a skilled tree surgeon to remove the lifeless wood and graft in vital new shoots. If so, watch out! Only recent recruits, untainted by the rot and eager to inject imagination into the revival of the business, may have a realistic hope of earning a better package of salary and retirement benefits.

Or is that an unnecessarily doleful picture? Surely there must be a happier way of putting it!

Justifying a better deal

If somebody is bidding to take over the company that employs you, it's up to you to show your mettle. Prove that you justify being retained as a key member of the team, who will contribute ideas that will help to transform the business.

You may often have wondered why the company was using what appeared to be antiquated systems that Noah would have discarded when he was building the ark. If so, you must have ideas about how the job could be done better. Put your ideas down on paper, and take them to one of the people who have come in to turn the business round.

Earn security and a bright future for yourself. You won't be climbing at the expense of your old colleagues. Your pro-active behaviour will benefit them, as well as you.

GAINING FROM HIVING OFF

Takeovers and amalgamations are not the only modern business phenomena. Successful enterprises diversify their interests. They find new uses for processes that they have already developed and new markets for established products. The diversity of the company's activities may become so great that the organisation is unwieldy.

Planning a reorganisation

The Board recognise the problem. They create a team of imaginative staff to examine the whole spread of the company's operations. They may add a specialist adviser, from outside, to co-ordinate the exercise and help the team to prepare a report. This will recommend what action the Board should take to maximise efficiency and profitability.

The likelihood of your being included in the team may be remote. But you may be among those members of staff who are asked questions by one of the team. Answer the questions as helpfully as you can. Respond in a way that will encourage further questions. The more you help the questioner to carry out his or her brief, the more likely you are to figure beneficially in the report.

Appointing trustees

As soon as the Board have decided to accept the proposals of the team, changes will start to be made. These may include the setting up of one or more new companies, either as subsidiaries of the original company or as independent but friendly new enterprises.

It may be appropriate to set up at least one new pension scheme. If so, trustees should be appointed, as soon as possible. The members must nominate at least a third of them. This may present a problem, when everything seems to be happening at once.

Gaining experience

Until the employees of the new company have been told who they are, they cannot nominate trustees. But it is highly desirable that token trustees should be able to see, and comment on, suggestions relating to a new pension scheme, as soon as they are made. *Be willing to be nominated as a stopgap trustee*, if anybody suggests you. Be willing to learn to be a good trustee. It will add to your usefulness and to your experience of dealing with problems from other people's points of view.

Dividing the pension fund

When details of which employees will stay with the original employer and who will move to a new employer are known, an actuary will need to receive full details. His or her task will be to:

- value the current assets and liabilities of the existing scheme

- recommend a division of assets between the schemes

- recommend future contributions to the schemes

- satisfy the PSO of the solvency of the schemes and the adequacy of the proposed contributions.

Because of the separate existence of the companies, it is desirable that separate actuarial reports should be made for each company, by independent actuaries.

Looking at morale

The action of the board of the original company in agreeing to the hiving off is evidence of their confidence in the continuing prosperity of their company. The board of the new company evidently has similar confidence. This should encourage both sets of employees to expect their employers to prosper.

CHECKLIST

- Always be alert to sense any impending change, whether it might lead to your employers':

  - amalgamating with another employer
  - being taken over by another employer
  - creating a subsidiary
  - hiving off from a parent or conglomerate.

- Let your superiors and your colleagues recognise the imaginative contribution you make to the progress of your employers.

9
Becoming Redundant

In 1946, hundreds of thousands of United Kingdom citizens were redundant. World War II had ended, and the armed forces no longer needed them. But a programme had been prepared for releasing them to find civilian jobs.

Few, if any, of those men and women thought of themselves as being redundant. That angle of their status never crossed their minds. They were impatient to return to civvy street. However, looking at that mass redistribution of employments in an unfamiliar way might help you to look at redundancy from more than one angle.

ASSESSING THE SITUATION

There are various degrees of severity in being made redundant. The secretary to an author becomes redundant if her employer decides to emigrate to Australia. The workforce of a company becomes redundant if the company becomes insolvent.

The secretary may quickly find a new employer. The members of the redundant workforce may encounter more difficulties. They are probably of many ages and skills, and they may be competing with many other people who are looking for jobs in the neighbourhood.

Registering for unemployment benefit

First things first. If you become redundant, visit your local Employment Service Job Centre and register yourself as unemployed. Lose no time in making contact. Claims cannot usually be backdated.

You have no reason to feel embarrassed and think that registering is *infra dig*. It is no fault of yours that you have been made redundant. But you do need the money. Don't try to live on your savings until you get another job. You don't know when that will be. Keep your savings in reserve.

Examining your finances

It is important to face facts as quickly as possible. Optimistic guesses are worse than useless. They give a false and misleading impression of one's real resources.

Settle down (with your partner, if you have one) and list your income and expenditure. The number of items of income is probably small and unlikely to take long to list. It should include whatever unemployment benefit you are likely to receive.

The list of expenditure will be longer. It should include all the items – not just the large ones. Figure 7 contains a memory-jogger in tabular form, to help you. It's a shattering number of items, isn't it?

Thinking about economy

By this time you may be thinking that you must have made a mistake somewhere. You can't have got those figures right, can you? Perhaps you used a credit card to buy some of the items. Oh dear! Had you forgotten that outstanding bill?

- Evidently the situation is worse than you feared.
- What are you going to do about it?
- Borrowing to pay off what you owe would make matters worse.
- You were spending more than your income.
- You **must** cut your expenditure.
- Where are you going to start?

Seeing a happier picture

Let's hope that you find a less gloomy situation than the one the previous subsection portrays. You discover that you had more or less been breaking even. That is less of a problem, but clearly you will still need to tighten your belt because of redundancy.

Most people tend to live up to their income. That appears to be human nature. But careful analysis will usually show that economies are possible for people with average or above average incomes, without causing too great hardship.

Taking a realistic line

Redundancy is a severe blow that often comes without warning. It is usually unaccompanied by any clue to where further employment may be found. In the circumstances, the only safe reaction for the victim is to economise.

We are all familiar with goods and services that most people regarded as luxuries, when first they became available. Today they are

Item	Annual cost
Mortgage or rent	
Car tax	
Car insurance	
Household insurance	
Life assurance	
Local government rates	
Electricity	
Gas	
Water rate	
Sewerage rate	
TV licence	
Cable TV	
Telephone	
Mobile phone	
Food	
Clothes	
Hairdressing	
Newspapers and magazines	
Entertainment	
Subscriptions	
National lottery	
Football pools	
Drinking	
Smoking	
Holidays	
Birthday presents	
Christmas presents	
Parties	
Children's pocket money	
Unlisted other items	
ditto	
TOTAL	

Fig. 7. Listing your annual expenditure.

looked on as necessities. Private cars and colour TV sets are obvious examples. Mobile phones are heading that way. People survived without them for many years. People who have suffered redundancy have learned to survive without them again.

Shopping wisely

Probably you and your family have responded to appeals by various charities to donate clothing, books and other items for sale in their shops. Have you ever browsed in those shops? Redundancy could be the spur to encourage you and your family to replace your clothes, when necessary, by buying good-as-new items at knockdown prices at charity shops.

There is another kind of shop that might be an asset to you, as you try to find your feet in a world where the streets are not paved with gold. It is a bookshop that fills its shelves and tables with books in mint condition. They are remainders – books that the publishers sold off cheaply, when the demand for them slackened.

Watching for the off-chance

There is nothing wrong with the books, except that nobody has bought them. Spend time in looking at them. That will cost you nothing, and you might find something among them that could increase your knowledge of a subject or a skill, that could help to qualify you for a new job.

SEEKING FURTHER EMPLOYMENT

The most effective action you can take, after plugging leaks in the economy, is to find another job. It is easy to say; it is far from easy to do. You must lose no time in starting the search.

You need to concentrate your efforts and to work at it as hard as you worked at your job. For the moment, **this is your job**.

Knowing yourself

You need to present yourself to a potential new employer as the right person to fill an important vacancy. To achieve this objective you must first remind yourself of the qualities that fit you for the job.

Settle yourself in a quiet corner, and make a note of all the qualifications and useful experience you have. At this stage you have no particular job in mind. You are searching your memory for anything noteworthy.

- It may be a course or conference you have attended.

- It may be a diploma or certificate you have earned by satisfying instructors or examiners of your competence.

- It may be a tricky problem you solved for an employer.

- It may be a new system you devised to speed up a vital process.

Applying the knowledge

Search for job vacancy advertisements that appear to fit your skills. You may find them in Job Centres, in local newspapers, in trade journals or the national press. The last of these is likely to attract a large number of applications. It may attract so many that the process of whittling them down to a short list for interviewing will be measured in months rather than weeks. If you do answer such an advertisement, you might be wise to apply elsewhere as well.

Before preparing a CV to send to an advertiser, study the advertisement carefully, searching for clues to precisely what is on offer. Try to provide the CV information in the way that will be most likely to convince the reader that you are the right person for the job.

Approaching an employment agency

You may wish to increase your scope for learning about job vacancies by contacting an employment agency. Some employers do all their recruiting by using them. The agencies should weed out the no-hopers and save employers the chore of ploughing through time-wasting CVs.

An agency charges the employer a fee for providing a service. So you should not need to pay the agency. If you are asked for a fee, the simplest response is to go to another agency.

BRUSHING UP YOUR SKILLS

While you are waiting to land a job to suit your abilities, update yourself on every aspect of the job you are trying to secure. Scan trade or professional journals for articles that might widen or deepen your knowledge of the subject.

Keep in touch with colleagues who are still with your old employer or are in the job queue with you. Talking to them, occasionally, can benefit both them and you. You can:

- encourage each other
- pass on helpful information to each other
- learn from each other.

GETTING A REDUNDANCY PAYMENT

To qualify for this kind of payment:

- you must be between 18 and 65 years old

- you must have been in this employment continuously for at least two years

- you must have worked for 16 hours or more, each week.

You want to get maximum benefit from the money. That goes without saying. Therefore you will want to stop and think about the future, before starting to part with your cash.

Using the payment

Start by answering this question. Is the money:

1. a payment for services rendered?
2. compensation for losing your job?
3. a little something to help to tide you over?

It is not taxable, so presumably 1 does not apply. Surely the money is a combination of 2 and 3. So you should use it to soften the blow and help with the immediate problems.

Have you any outstanding debts? Paying them off could ease the strain.

You know how big the gap is between your income and expenditure, after you have made all the reasonable economies. For how long would you redundancy payment bridge that gap? If the answer fills you with horror, you would be wise to take a look at where you might economise further.

CHECKING ON YOUR PENSION SCHEME RIGHTS

If you have been a member of your employer's pension scheme for less than two years, you may be able to take a refund of any contributions you have made. Because you will have been allowed income tax relief on the contributions, tax will be deducted from the refund.

If you have been a member for two years or more, no such refunds are allowable, but you will be entitled to preservation of retirement and death benefits payable in accordance with the rules of the scheme.

Questioning the security

If your employer is making people redundant, how safe are their rights under the pension scheme?

You naturally want to ask that question. The best people to address it to are the trustees of the scheme. They are responsible for keeping an eye on the security of the pension fund. They receive regular reports and recommendations from the scheme's actuary and check that the employer has carried out the recommendations.

Having benefits bought out

Becoming redundant is, for many purposes, another change of employment to add to those mentioned in Chapters 7 and 8. The option of having a transfer payment made to a new employer's scheme, an appropriate personal pension or a section 32 policy is available. Whether this is an appropriate time to exercise it is a moot point.

The actuary who would have to calculate the transfer value would have reason to be extra cautious in making assumptions. At a time of possible uncertainty about the employer's future, it would be wrong to risk prejudicing the members whose jobs were not being touched – yet.

By the same tokens, should someone who was already redundant grab what he or she could get, while the going was good? There is no watertight answer to that question.

Being reinstated

One of the factors that prevents a watertight answer is the possibility that the situation that led to the redundancies may blow over, after a few months or a couple of years. Having weathered the storm, the employer may be keen to regain the services of the most competent of those who were given the push when times were bad.

Some of them may have found new employment elsewhere; some may be reluctant to return to an employer who has jettisoned them once before. Some may be confident that the old employer is now established more surely, and that they would be happier to return to a business they know well than to remain with a relatively unknown new employer.

Accruing additional pension scheme benefits

The PSO is happy, in the circumstances, for the returning employees to start accruing benefits under the employer's pension scheme again. For example, Gordon Roberts is a member of BCDE Plc's pension scheme. It provides a pension of 1/60th of final remuneration for each year of service, from normal pension age. After completing 12 years' service, he is made redundant.

Two years later, Gordon is invited to rejoin the company. Every year of his new period of service with the company will be added to the 12 years of his previous service, in calculating his total pensionable service. The whole of that total will provide 60ths of final remuneration in calculating his eventual pension.

STOPPING CONTRIBUTIONS TO A PERSONAL PENSION

Peter Green is employed by a company that has no pension scheme. To make up for that omission, to some extent, he contributes to a personal pension, making maximum permissible payments each year. If he is made redundant, his earnings cease, until such time as he finds another source of earnings. In the interim he has nothing to justify his contributing to a personal pension.

TREATING REDUNDANCY AS EARLY RETIREMENT

If you have reached the age of 50 when you become redundant, you might decide to treat your joblessness as early retirement. It is permissible, but is it a good idea?

If:

- you realise that you cannot draw your state pension until state pension age

- you have paid off your mortgage

- your children are off your hands

- you have an adequate additional source of income to supplement your reduced pension

- you have enough rewarding pursuits to occupy your time fully and

- your partner, if any, does not object to having you under his/her feet for much of the day

you might make a go of it. But before you make any decisions, ponder some words from Shakespeare:

'If all the year were playing holidays,
To sport would be as tedious as to work.'

(Henry IV Part 1 Act 1 Scene 2)

Idleness is no less boring in the reign of Elizabeth II.

Making an irrevocable decision

You may recall reading that one can postpone drawing one's state pension after starting to draw it. (The option can be exercised only once.) There is no similar option in an occupational pension scheme. Once payment of your pension has begun, it continues for the rest of your life.

If you start to draw your pension early, the amount you draw, each month, is less than it would have been if you had waited until normal pension age. That is only to be expected. If the money is spread further, it must be spread more thinly. And the money has been in the pension fund for fewer years in which to earn interest.

Looking before you leap

There are times when that irrevocable decision may be the right one. One cannot usually retire early unless one is at least 50 years old. Many people who have passed that age have started to think about what they hope to do in retirement. Some of them are likely to plan to do a part-time job. If it were reasonably well paid, it could top-up an early retirement pension to equal or exceed the pre-retirement earnings.

Interpreting part-time flexibly

Frank was a bank clerk who had taken early retirement. A farmer friend asked Frank whether he would be willing to help him out with his book-keeping. Frank agreed to 'give it a go' and quickly mastered the job, devoting one day a week to it. His fee made a useful addition to his pension, and Frank did not hesitate to accept the invitation, when one of the farmer's neighbours asked if Frank could provide the same service for him.

By the end of 12 months, Frank had added three further clients to his list, and speeded up his method of working enough to leave every afternoon free for recreation. The gilt on the gingerbread was that Frank's pension plus his earnings had topped his pre-retirement salary by a useful margin.

It would be stupid to suggest that every reader of this book could emulate Frank's example, but this true story might give you a clue to how you might apply your own skills profitably.

CHECKLIST

- Your priorities, immediately you become redundant, must be to:
    - register yourself as unemployed
    - assess your financial resources and expenses
    - cut your expenditure
    - leave your retirement benefits with your ex-employer's pension scheme
    - actively seek further employment.

- When you have those priorities in train, you should devote your energies to:
    - finding further employment for which you have the skills
    - improving your existing skills
    - acquiring other skills that job vacancy advertisements show to be in demand
    - finding employment for your new skills.

10
Reaching Retirement

Retirement is a milestone – not a finishing post. Ideally it is also the junction between two rewarding periods of a person's life – the meeting point of:

- the years in which one lives on a salary or wages that are the reward for the job one is doing and

- the years in which one lives on retirement benefits that are a reward for what one did during one's working years.

Choosing the form in which one will receive those benefits deserves careful thought.

RECOGNISING CONFLICTING FACTORS

Until recent years, many occupational pension schemes had normal pension ages of 65 and 60 for men and women respectively. These matched the state pension ages.

Then equal opportunities legislation introduced a requirement that men and women should be treated alike. The prospect of having to pay state pensions to men at 60 instead of 65 appalled politicians, so they approved legislation to move the state pension age for women, progressively, to 65 (see Chapter 1). The state pension date for every woman who was born after 5 April 1950 will be later than her 60th birthday.

Many employers reacted differently. They reduced the normal pension age for men to 60. So, for the foreseeable future, many people will qualify for an occupational pension five years earlier than for the state pension.

CONSIDERING AVAILABLE OPTIONS

Although the part of the Inland Revenue that deals with pension schemes is called the Pension Schemes Office, the Practice Notes contain frequent references to 'retirement benefits schemes' and 'relevant benefits'. In other words, it is recognised that a pension is not the only financial reward that people look for when they retire from employment.

Commuting pension for a lump sum

This is the option that appeals most strongly to most people, as their last day in the shop, office or factory approaches. They think that it is the next best thing to winning the lottery or the pools. They believe that there is an established tradition that one can take a quarter of one's pension as a tax-free lump sum. People see this as a 'Welcome Home' light at the end of a long road.

Noting the true amount

The reference to a quarter of the pension tends to be an approximation, for most people. It stems from a time-honoured feature of the pension scheme for members of the Civil Service. The basic formula that the PSO's Practice Notes quote as the maximum lump sum is '3/80ths of final remuneration for each year of service – up to 40 years'. When you are approaching retirement, the person responsible for your employer's scheme will give you details of the precise amounts of your pension, maximum lump sum, and the amount by which your taking that sum would reduce your pension.

Counting the cost

By quoting that information to you, that person has discharged his or her responsibility. But you need to see those figures in real terms – in relation to the way they may affect the rest of your life.

You may see them in the context of an ambition that you and your partner have dreamed about. You have been promising each other that the lump sum would pay for a memorable cruise to the Bahamas. You both feel that, as long as the lump sum will be large enough to pay for the cruise and to buy some souvenirs of the holiday, you will be happy.

Looking ahead

The last thing you want, at such an exciting moment, is for somebody to suggest that you should look at the long-term cost of your proposed trip. You know the cost of the package holiday. There it is in the travel agent's brochure.

But that is the short-term cost. Surely you should look also at the effect that sacrificing part of your pension would have on your standard of living in future years. Before you commit yourself to taking the cruise, or even to taking the lump sum, settle down with a large sheet of paper and list your annual expenditure.

Facing facts

You may find that difficult. You have not been in the habit of keeping track of where the money goes. All you know is that, by the time each pay day arrives, the kitty is empty. In that case, the problem is easy to solve. You know what you earn now. You have been told what your pension will be, *without your sacrificing part of it to provide the lump sum*. Obviously you are going to need to tighten your belt a bit. Think how much more difficult it would be if you had to live on a reduced pension, having sacrificed the remainder.

Saving some expenses

Many people save on some expenses when they no longer go to a job, each day. They save the train or bus fares that had cost them a substantial amount, and the casual clothes they wear in their relaxed lifestyle may be inexpensive. Eating lunch at home is cheaper than eating out, too.

These economies all help to bridge the gap between your income before and after retirement. But there is still a gap, and it would be wider if you took that lump sum and spent it.

Being prudent with a lump sum

When somebody is relying on commuting part of his or her pension to pay for a cruise, it suggests that the cruise would be completely out of the question, if the lump sum were not available to pay for it. So how would the pensioner fare if an unforeseen expense cropped up, when the cruise had ended? Perhaps there is a better way to use a lump sum.

It is always useful to have a nest-egg tucked away somewhere, that you can turn to in an emergency. You may already know that, from experience. Your lump sum, in place of part of your pension, could be just such a nest-egg.

Minimising the drop in income

You wouldn't keep it in cash, of course. You would put it in a deposit account with a building society or a bank. That would earn you interest, as well as taking care of your lump sum. In that way it would provide you with an additional income to supplement your pension.

And the lump sum would still be available if you needed it in an emergency.

Clearing the decks first

Before making any other use of the lump sum, you need to check that you have no debts to clear. If you have been buying your house or flat by means of a mortgage, you should get a quotation for paying off any outstanding amount. The rate of interest you pay on the mortgage (or on any other loan) is higher than the rate you will receive on your deposit account.

Looking at another possibility

One opportunity you may know nothing about is worth exploring. It entails taking the largest lump sum you can have and using it to buy an annuity. It may look mad, but there is method in the madness.

Its effectiveness derives from the difference between how income tax is levied on a pension and on a 'purchased life annuity' (PLA).

A PLA is a policy, bought from a life assurance company or a friendly society out of the purchaser's own money. The policy provides an income payable during the remainder of the purchaser's life. Figure 8 illustrates how the amount of tax payable on this income differs from the tax payable on a pension of the same amount.

Looking at a rarely used option

It is most unusual for a member who is retiring to decide that he or she would like to make provision for someone who is dependent on the member by reason of a physical or mental handicap. The reason why the provision of such a pension is unusual may be that few scheme members are aware of the facility.

Although PSO Practice Note 12.5 says that 'an employee may surrender part of his or her own pension to provide a pension for a dependant, to commence on his or her death after retirement,' scheme members' booklets may not mention the facility. Chapter 6 gives further details. They may merit your attention.

BRINGING OTHER ASSETS INTO THE PICTURE

Your membership of the pension scheme is an important asset. It is probably by no means your only asset. You would be wise to take all of them into consideration, when deciding what to do about the option to receive a lump sum instead of part of your pension.

When Charles Thomson retired on his 60th birthday, his employer's pension scheme provided Charles with a pension of £5,000 a year.

Also on that birthday, Charles bought himself an annuity of £5,000 a year from a life assurance company. He found that, while only about half of the annuity was treated as income, for tax purposes, the whole of his pension was treated as income.

How does this come about?

In his Budget Speech in 1956, the then Chancellor of the Exchequer agreed that, when somebody buys an annuity from a life assurance company, each payment of the annuity consists partly of interest on the purchase money and partly of a refund of a portion of the purchase money. That refund should *not* be taxed. It is a capital payment.

If Charles had waited until his 70th birthday before buying the annuity, an even smaller part of each payment would have been taxed. The life office would have had fewer years in which to refund the purchase money.

Fig. 8. The difference between the income tax payable on an occupational pension and on an annuity bought by the recipient.

Assessing the importance of your home

Whether you own your home or rent it, it is an asset – at least in one sense of the word. But is it still appropriate to your circumstances? Maybe your household has diminished since you moved in, many years ago. Would something smaller suit you better, now? Would you be better off with a flat or a bungalow? It would probably be easier to keep clean, and cost you less for heating and rent or rates.

Another point you might like to consider is the convenience of where your home is. You may have enjoyed the walk to the station, every morning, as you went to wherever you worked. Would you and your partner be happier to live nearer the shops, now?

Looking at your furnishings and decorations

If you are happy with the house, itself, would it be a good idea to fit a new carpet on the stairs? Badly worn carpets are hazards for anybody who catches a heel in a bad patch. And how about buying new armchairs that would give your partner and you better comfort and support? You are active and alert now, but increasingly you will appreciate such improvements.

In a few years' time you may have greater difficulty in making changes, such as these. Giving yourselves a good start in your new way of life can pay handsome dividends.

Another aspect of this philosophy is looking at where all your electric appliances are plugged in. How many adaptors are you using, so that two or more items use the same socket? And how many sockets are in difficult places to reach? Having an electrician to sort things out now could avoid fractured wrists or ankles in a few years' time if somebody tripped over the lead to an electrical appliance.

Making the most of the opportunity
Inertia is such a potent state that one should seize the opportunity, that such an event as retiring offers, for getting desirable things done. Provided that they are genuine and desirable improvements, they can be achieved more economically while everything else is being done.

ENSURING THAT YOU AND YOUR PARTNER ARE AGREED

Beware of the avalanche effect! As soon as retirement becomes an important issue on the domestic agenda, make sure that, if you have a partner, the two of you discuss and agree each step. This will enable each of you to apply the brakes to the other's wild ideas. It will also ensure that you can improve each other's good ideas.

TAKING ACCOUNT OF DIFFERING PENSION DATES

If both you and your partner are members of occupational pension schemes, each of you is likely to have occupational and state pensions starting on different dates. You may have as many as four start-dates between you. You may be able to fit those dates into a joint plan to finance your combined transition from employee to pensioner status.

DEALING WITH DISSATISFACTION

It would be surprising if nobody ever found a reason to complain about his or her pension, when the time came to start drawing it. Often such complaints stem from the member's having misread the rules or the statements that have been issued about benefits. Sometimes Jack has relied on what Charlie told him about the scheme, and Charlie has a flair for getting hold of the wrong end of any stick that is offered to him.

Asking the right people

If you disagree with what you are told that you are entitled to receive, when your retirement is approaching, raise the matter with the appropriate person. If you are concerned about your occupational pension, write or speak to the manager of the scheme or to one of the trustees. They are responsible for seeing that the scheme operates properly.

If your problem relates to a personal pension, write to the life assurance company, friendly society, unit trust group or other approved provider responsible for paying the pension.

If you do not get satisfaction, consult the list of useful addresses at the back of this book. Choose the one that appears most likely to be able to help, and write a letter setting out the situation as clearly and fully as you can.

CHECKLIST

- Take stock, with your partner (if any), of:
  - any outstanding mortgage or other borrowing
  - whether you ought to move to a different home
  - whether any furnishings need to be replaced
  - whether your electricity points are adequate and well sited.

- Decide (with your partner – if any):
  - how your income after retirement will compare with your present income
  - how your expenditure after retirement will compare with your present expenditure
  - how you should allocate whatever lump sum you take, in lieu of pension, among:
      clearing any outstanding loans;
      buying a Purchased Life Annuity;
      starting a deposit account with a bank or building society;
      spending on refurnishing your home.

11
Enjoying Retirement

There is more to a rewarding retirement than having a comfortable income. The money may enable you to be miserable in comfort, but who wants to be miserable?

PLANNING WELL IN ADVANCE

When you wake up on the morning after your last day at work, welcome the first day of your retirement with a smile. Make sure that your partner has good reason to be glad that you will not be rushing off to work, every morning, in future. Let him or her see that you are going to be an asset at home.

This change of lifestyle is not something that comes automatically. Like any other change of direction, it needs planning. You need to apply the brakes gently and ease into the arrival platform. Crashing into the buffers is a painful way of reaching the terminus. People whose careers end abruptly, by reason of redundancy or ill health, are unfortunate. Take full advantage of the period of notice you have of the approach of retirement.

Overdoing it?
Theoretically that means you should start planning now, even if you have been in your job for a few months only. If you know that the normal pension age for your job is 60, and your last birthday was your 25th, you have 34 years in which to plan for retirement.

That would be a bit over the top, for most purposes. But if your employer's pension scheme provides benefits that are less than the maxima that the PSO would approve, the earlier you start making AVCs or FSAVCs, the better.

In the absence of that reason for starting as early as possible, beginning to plan for retirement between five and ten years in advance should be adequate.

Sharing ideas

Discuss the retirement scenario with your partner. You should plan it together. Make sure that it suits and pleases each of you.

Think of all the opportunities the new status offers to each of you. List things that each of you would like to do but have been prevented from doing, as long as there has been a daily round that you have needed to follow.

Have a mix of activities that you can enjoy together, but make sure that you each have some activities that the other does not share. Be realistic. Avoid being so intent on doing everything together that the survivor will be completely lost when one of you reaches the end of the road.

Being flexible

Avoid falling into the trap of thinking that your plans must be set in stone. Keep your minds active and ready to receive new ideas. But beware of either of you changing a plan without discussing it with the other. Each of you must know when the other thinks that there may be a better way of dealing with a situation.

Subject to that proviso, you should welcome new slants on situations and novel approaches to problems. One of the secrets of ageing happily is keeping one's mind active.

KEEPING FIT

'Mr Smith, isn't it wonderful about the test match?'

The speaker was 93 years old, and he was making use of the players' lunch break to take his daily constitutional. He was striding out as if he were 40 years younger. He was determined to keep both mind and body active, and he was enjoying watching other people living actively, as well as living actively himself.

Keeping fit is a positive activity. It means getting up, each morning, with a day of activity in front of you, and going to bed, each evening, with the knowledge of having achieved something worthwhile.

Achieving variety and moderation

'Variety's the very spice of life
That gives it all its flavour.'

William Cowper, the British poet, wrote those words nearly 200 years ago, but they are still true today.

Variety in what you do with yourself each day certainly adds spice to your life. Following the same routine, day after day, is a recipe for boredom.

Jeffrey was a clerk in an office where he had worked ever since he left school. He had lunch in the same restaurant each day, and always chose the same items from the menu. Six months before he was due to draw his pension, he cut his spending to what his income would be in retirement. Apart from that, his routine remained unaltered. Three months later, he failed to wake up one morning. Boredom had taken its toll.

Eating and drinking

One might say that Jeffrey's way of life lacked moderation as well as variety. It is more usual to counsel moderation in the context of food and alcohol. Certainly a doctor carrying out medical examinations for life assurance purposes takes a dim view of over indulgence in food or alcohol. Either can harm one's health.

Alcohol tends to attract more attention than overeating. This is probably because of its featuring in road casualty statistics. 'Don't drink and drive' posters are familiar to all of us. But a non-driver who drinks heavily, particularly spirits, adds to his or her health hazards.

Smoking

For at least 40 years, most members of the medical profession have been drawing attention to the effect that tobacco smoking can have on health. Progressively, research has added passive smoking to active smoking as a source of physical deterioration. The time has surely passed when people could throw serious doubt on the declared health hazard of being in the company of smokers, let alone indulging in their habit.

It appears that a large proportion of the people in the UK who were smokers, before reliable statistics about the effect of smoking on health were published, have broken the tobacco habit. Yet large numbers of children are succumbing to the habit at an early age. Mercifully, increasing numbers of shops, offices, restaurants, bars and trains are banning smoking.

It is too early to know how these factors will combine to affect the longevity of tomorrow's pensioners.

CHOOSING WHERE TO LIVE

How much thought have you given to where you would like to live, when you have retired? The question deserves careful consideration. You may have been pushing it under the carpet. If there is any reason why you expect to want to move to somewhere more convenient for life in retirement, do something about it now. You will never be as young again.

Thinking about moving

Some people have spent many happy holidays at a picturesque village by the sea. They have been there so often that they:

- know several of the residents well
- have enjoyed long chats with them
- have even talked about living there in retirement.

Many people have bought a seaside house, on the strength of such memories. Some of them have soon regretted their decision. The cost of two moves, in quick succession, has made a big hole in their capital.

Trying it out

If you are confident that you and your partner could achieve a happier result, how about renting a house or bungalow in your pet village, out of season? Take it for at least a fortnight in midwinter, and rely on buying all your food at local shops. That should give you a better idea of what being a resident is like. If there is a blizzard during your stay, that will be a bonus.

Looking ahead

You may have been thinking that the house you live in is larger than you need. Quitting the rat race will give you a chance to move without having to choose somewhere convenient for commuting.

That seems a good idea. While you are about it, might you be wise to bear in mind that household chores can become increasingly irksome, as the years go by. Would a bungalow or a flat be a welcome replacement for the house you are living in?

And, bearing in mind that successive governments are apparently going to do their utmost to drive private cars off the roads, accessibility of bus routes and railway stations is going to be at a premium.

MIXING WITH MORE PEOPLE

The people you work with may be a more important part of your environment than you realise. You are going to miss the little chats you have had with some of them – a few words, here or there about this or that. They are part of life. As John Donne said, 'No man is an island, entire of itself'.

Passing the time of day or commenting briefly on the weather is better than nothing. Making the postman feel that he is more than just somebody who shoves letters through a slot in the door, and rings the bell if they are too big, can brighten his day.

Attending local meetings

Going to meetings at your local town or village hall occasionally could widen your circle of acquaintance. It does not matter whether you agree with the speakers or not. You are showing an interest and widening your knowledge of what other people think.

Joining a local group of some kind

There are many groups that one could join. There must be something that interests you. Look at the list held by your local library. Figure 9 quotes the groups named on one such list. You can see what a range of interests it covers. Joining such a group would put you in touch with interesting people whom you would probably not have met, otherwise. It would also make *you* more interesting, by widening your scope for conversation.

DEVELOPING NEW INTERESTS

Make ageing an illusion by exploring new subjects with youthful enthusiasm. There are many ways in which you can do this. Go to the lending department of your public library and look at the books in the non-fiction area.

There are books about hundreds of subjects. Pick one that you know nothing about and choose a book that looks as if it is intended to help beginners. Take it home, make yourself comfortable in a chair, with the book and a dictionary, and start to read.

If one of the words floors you, look it up in the dictionary. Keep on reading for at least an hour. If the subject is boring you, by the end of that time, try to find another book about it that looks more hopeful. If that one fails to capture your interest, too, try another subject.

Active Retirement Association	Lions Club
Amateur Radio Society	Local History Society
Art Society	Marquetry Group
Astronomical Society	Model Boat Club
Baroque Singers	Model Railway Club
Beekeepers Association	Music Club
Bridge Club	Operatic and Dramatic Society
British Legion	Pensioners Association
Camera Club	Philatelic Society
Campaign for Nuclear Disarmament	Poetry Society
Canine Society	Probus Club
Chess Club	Radio Flyers
Choral Society	Rotary Club
Computer Club	Soroptimist International
Decorative & Fine Arts Society	Theatregoers Club
Embroiderers Guild	Townswomens Guild
Family History Society	Winemakers Circle
Film Society	Womens Institute
Kite Club	Writers Circle

Fig. 9. A list of local clubs and societies compiled by a public library.

Increasing your scope

You may soon find that your local library has no recent books on the subject you have started to study. There may be more up-to-date books in another branch of the county library. Each main branch has a catalogue of all the books owned by the county. This has three elements:

1. an index to the numerical classification of subjects
2. a file of microfiches
3. a viewer.

The index is alphabetical and is usually divided into several volumes, such as A-D, E-K, L-R and S-Z. A typical entry is shown in Figure 10.

If you wanted to discover what books about pension schemes were held in your county's libraries, you would need to remove the **microfiche** that included classification 331.252 from the file and insert it in the viewer. Each microfiche contains details of a large

Pensions – Civil Service

– central governments		351.5
– employment law		344.01252
"	***	344.012
– executive management		658.407253
"	***	658.407
– labour economics		331.252
– social security		368.43

*** old numbers – no longer used

Fig. 10. Specimen entry in index of numerical classifications of subjects.

number of books, in minute letters and numerals.

Figure 11 shows an example of the information recorded about one title under subject 331.252 on a microfiche in the catalogue for Kent County Library.

Toulson Norman		331.252
The Pensions Revolution: An Employer's Guide		PBK
Kogan Page	1988	88/32
1850917647		
Dover A	Maidstone A	T Wells A
Tonbridge R		

The ten digit number is the International Standard Book Number. The information in the subsequent lines indicates the branch libraries that hold copies of the book. The letter 'R' indicates that the copy at Tonbridge library is in the reference section and not available for borrowing. It can be referred to only in the reading room.

Fig. 11. Specimen microfiche information in Kent County Library catalogue.

Borrowing a book

You may find that there is a copy of a book you would like to borrow in a branch that is reasonably easy for you to visit. You can then go and collect it. If the only available copies are farther afield, your local branch will be happy to obtain one from the holding library for you, for a small fee.

Adding to your personal library

As your interest in a subject grows, you may be glad to create your own handy store of relevant information by selecting and collecting books about it. An occasional browse in a local bookshop may discover new works that you were unaware of. It may also whet your appetite for other subjects that could interest you.

Another excellent way to widen your interests is to join a carefully chosen book club. There are plenty to choose from, and some of them do not impose a requirement for you to buy a minimum number of choices within a stated period. Keep an eye open for book club advertisements, and read the terms of membership before committing yourself.

Varying your kind of reading

Avoid getting stuck in a rut. If you never read non-fiction or always read it, you cramp your enjoyment of reading. You will be better equipped to enjoy your retirement if you switch from non-fiction to fiction, and back to non-fction, from time to time. And both Agatha Christie and P D James are worthy of inclusion in your choice of crime stories, as are Dick Francis and Colin Dexter. But it would equally be wrong to ignore Elizabeth Jane Howard and Joanna Trollope because they do not write whodunits. Aim to be a well-rounded reader.

DOING VOLUNTARY WORK

There are plenty of outlets for anybody who is willing to devote some time to helping others, on a regular or occasional basis. It is a rewarding way of meeting and helping various kinds of people in various kinds of situation. And if you have difficulty in relating to people on a one to one basis, there are opportunities for helping people whom you never meet.

Examples of two different styles of work are provided by:

- people who use their own cars to ferry moderately immobile people to visit friends or relatives who are in hospital (the cost of petrol being repaid)

* people who help to provide 'talking newspapers' for the blind by reading from local newspapers to a tape recorder. (Many copies are made of the tape and distributed to the people who need them.)

The scope for this kind of activity is enormous and constantly expanding, as perceptive and imaginative people discover needs that have passed unnoticed.

Finding suitable voluntary work

You may find the address of the nearest volunteer bureau in your local telephone directory. The manager will be pleased to meet you and tell you about organisations who would appreciate your help.

Local newspapers and freebies sometimes contain news items about the services that various groups are providing, and their need for recruits. Local radio stations also broadcast details of organisations that need help. And the people who hold collecting boxes, seeking aid for charities, will usually be happy to tell you something of the work of those charities. You need never find yourself at a loose end, if you keep your eyes and ears open.

ADDING TO YOUR SKILLS

None of us has exhausted the scope for gaining knowledge. It may be that we could usefully learn how to do some of our own decorating, or repairing damage when it occurs in our home.

Possibly we might enjoy a holiday in France more if we could speak the language.

Those are only a few of the numerous subjects about which many of us are ignorant. Closing some of the gaps can be a rewarding way of occupying some of the time that retirement makes available.

Looking at local facilities

Local educational authorities arrange training facilities for people of many ambitions and all ages. They usually publish a booklet, listing the available subjects and locations, and the dates and cost of attending. They often make preferential charges for senior citizens.

The courses offered range widely. They usually include:

- academic subjects, such as modern maths, languages and history

- manual skills such as carpentry, pottery and metal working

- domestic skills, such as cookery, cake icing and dressmaking

- keep-fit activities such as yoga and aerobics

- appreciation of art, music and literature.

Prospectuses are usually available in July/August at public libraries, education offices and some bookshops.

Finding out about U3A

What is U3A? It is the University of the Third Age, but don't let the word 'university' put you off. The third age is the age of retirement – the age when, freed from the discipline of regular working hours, one may still have a lot going for one.

U3A is 'a self-help organisation to which each member brings his or her own particular knowledge or skill or enthusiasm'. There are more than 340 local U3As in the UK. In each of them, separate groups of about ten members meet in the home of one of the members to discuss and explore a subject in which they share a common interest. Depending on the subject, a group may meet for a few weeks only or for a longer period.

There are also monthly meetings, with guest speakers. These are open to all members. And there are occasional coach trips to places of cultural, historical or educational interest.

Noting the cost

The annual subscription is small. The cost of going on a coach trip would, of course, be additional.

TAKING HOLIDAYS

Life in retirement is not one long holiday, as some people suggest. Nor should it be. Satisfaction comes from achievement – not from indolence. But an occasional period of relaxation can help one to recharge one's batteries.

In this context 'relaxation' does not necessarily mean sitting or lying down, doing nothing. Going for a walk, away from one's usual environment, can be a form of relaxation.

Choosing where to go

Taking a holiday need not imply flying away to the Costa Brava, the Bahamas or Hawaii. It could be staying at a B & B for a couple of nights, near the sea, in the country, or in a quiet village, 15 miles from where you live. It could be staying with a relative or a friend.

Where you go and how long you stay there are less important than the action of taking a break. Choose those variables to suit your pocket.

STAYING IN TOUCH

When people leave their workplaces for the last time, when retirement arrives, they *sometimes* heave a great sigh of relief and say to themselves, 'Well that's that. I'm never going there again, thank goodness'. If that should happen to you, don't let it be your last word on the subject.

Whatever it was that caused you to feel like that, it would be a pity to let a tactless remark or an ill-considered comment sour a relationship. You might be glad to consult your ex-employer, one day, or he might invite you to help him to sort out a situation that had developed during your career. A payment for a few hours' work never comes amiss, when one is living on a pension.

Your employer may arrange facilities for retired members of the staff to meet socially, from time to time. Take advantage of these opportunities to have a chat. You never know what stresses some of the people there may be under. The chance to speak to somebody with a smiling face may be a tonic for someone who has recently suffered a bereavement.

CHECKLIST

- If you have less than ten years to go until your normal retirement age, you (and your partner – if any) need to start planning for its arrival.

- Various circumstances may change, between now and then. You will need to take account of them.

- Make a note in your diary to review your plans at intervals of a year or less, and to make appropriate changes.

- There is no need for you to wait until retirement has arrived before starting to pay attention to keeping fit, and widening your interests.

- *The more you implement your plans **before retirement arrives,** the more easily you will take to your change of status.*

12
Obtaining Independent Advice

Nobody can put a hand on his or her heart and swear that the advice he or she offers you is infallible. It is as well that you should know this, from the outset. Always bear it in mind when somebody is assuring you that the advice you are receiving is the best you can have.

BEING FRANK ABOUT YOUR RESOURCES AND YOUR OBJECTIVE

You want an adviser to give you an honest opinion about how you should approach your future. In that case, you must be frank about your resources and what you want to achieve. An open discussion of assets and objectives will put him or her on their mettle to point you in the right direction – at the right price.

Be alert, throughout your discussion(s) to pick up any hint that you may not be on the same wavelength. Draw the adviser's attention to this. Otherwise you may be to blame for any misdirection in the eventual plan for your pension.

CHECKING THE RELIABILITY OF POSSIBLE ADVISERS

Are there trustworthy ways of deciding whether the advice somebody offers you is likely to deserve your attention? There are pointers that can help you.

First among these is knowing who employs the would-be adviser. An employee of a pension provider, whether it be a life assurance company, a unit trust, or some other approved pension provider, has a duty to influence business in the direction of that employer. That is what he or she is employed to do. Recommending any other provider would be a breach of that duty, and could have dire consequences.

In that case, why do people do business with such an adviser? Sometimes it is because the employer has done all the insurance for

113

the client's family since goodness only knows when. There is a long-established connection.

Paying for service

At other times the adviser has approached the purchaser and done him or her a favour by persuading them to make some provision for retirement. That is a genuine service for someone who would otherwise have made no such provision. That persuasion deserves a reward. Although the purchaser might have found a more advantageous pension arrangement elsewhere, nobody took the trouble to suggest it.

Needing independent advice

Where can one find such advice?

There have been insurance brokers, stockbrokers and other independent financial advisers for as long as anybody who is in the insurance industry or investment world today can remember. Some of the advisers have been better than others.

Unfortunately some of them have deserved to be called 'commission chasers', instead of advisers. Their attitude has not been, 'How can I help this man to get the policy or investment he ought to have?' but, 'What can I persuade this man to buy through my agency?'

You may have read news items, in your daily paper, about such people pushing men and women who had changed their jobs into acting unwisely over their pension rights. Because of this, some life offices have had to recompense thousands of people who had been talked into doing the wrong thing.

Seeking reliable advice

Obviously there must be advisers who honestly strive to give sound advice to people who consult them. That is the objective of professional independent advisers. They study the principles of the branch of life assurance with which they are concerned, they satisfy examiners that they are fit people to be admitted to membership of one of the bodies that is mentioned in the list of useful addresses, at the end of this book. They keep abreast of developments. They try to ensure that they have a true picture of a client's needs and recommend the right contract with the right pension provider.

Looking at statutory control

In recent years various steps have been taken to tighten the supervision of the various people who are concerned with dealing with securities and investments. They have improved the situation. But one of the first statements that Gordon Brown made in Parliament, after being appointed Chancellor of the Exchequer in May 1997, announced his intention to reform financial regulation.

The process of reform has started. The Securities and Investments Board had been in existence for several years, overseeing the work of self-regulatory organisations that dealt with various aspects of the financial world. On 28 October 1997 it changed its name to the Financial Services Authority.

Figure 12 contains a list of the names and functions of the organisations that will make up the Financial Services Authority. Their addresses are listed at the end of this book.

Working in a changing environment

One has to accept that nobody can guarantee to be 100 per cent up-to-date in every detail, all the time. That is as true of independent pensions advisers as it is of anybody who relies on a file of facts when giving an opinion on the best line for a client to take.

The Financial Services Authority (FSA)
    Overseeing the regulatory system, regulating investment business and supervising exchanges and clearing houses
Building Societies Commission
    Building Societies
Registry of Friendly Societies
    Credit Unions and Mutual Societies
Friendly Societies Commission
    Friendly Societies
Supervision and Surveillance Division of the Bank of England
    Banks and the Wholesale Money Market Regime
Insurance Directorate of the Department of Trade and Industry
    Insurance Companies
Investment Management Regulatory Organisation (IMRO)
    Investment Management
Personal Investment Authority (PIA)
    Retail Investment Business (pensions, life assurance etc)
Securities and Futures Authority (SFA)
    Securities and Futures Business

Fig. 12. Organisations that will constitute the Financial Services Authority **and the financial sectors they cover**

Pension fund investment managers spend their lives assessing where they should invest their funds, so as to achieve the highest return, compatible with security. With this in mind, they study each day's news, alert to spot any item that might affect the profitability of certain industries or individual companies within those industries.

Some managers are more perceptive than their rivals in seeing and reading the clues to future gains and losses. If such a manager moves from fund A to fund B or suffers a heart attack or other debilitating condition, pensions advisers may need to adjust the 'league tables' that they use when making recommendations to clients. The purpose of any such adjustment is to take account of an estimated likely change in investment skill in the management of one or more funds.

Choosing an independent financial adviser

How does one start? There is no infallible answer to that question.

A personal recommendation may be reliable, if you have good reason to trust the judgement of the person who makes it. Otherwise it could be based on the opinion of a gullible person who has been taken in by 'such a charming young man', and has yet to discover that the charm was a veneer.

To be on the safe side, you would be wise to have mental reservations about any adviser who is recommended to you, until you have made your own assessment.

- Do you have any misgivings about an over-ready smile?
- Do you feel any pressure on you to commit yourself?
- Are you hearing facile arguments or cautious logic?
- Have you an uneasy feeling about this person?

Unless you are completely happy with the recommended adviser, make your exit as quickly as you can, and consult somebody else.

Looking at a list

Your local *Yellow Pages* probably contains a long list of financial advisers, but how are you to pick the right name from the list? Some of them mention that they are members of the British Insurance and Investment Brokers Association. That is a professional body that requires its members to qualify for admission. Others say that they are Regulated by the Personal Investment Authority. That is one of the bodies that were set up under the Financial Services Act 1986 to regulate those services. Each of those bodies tries to look after the interests of investors.

Asking about the cost

Advisers expect to receive payment for the service they provide. There is nothing wrong in that. They charge a fee that is based on how much time they devote to:

- assessing what you tell them about your circumstances
- taking note of your objective(s)
- deciding how best to advise you
- providing you with a reasoned recommendation
- arranging the agreed pension provision for you.

If asked about their fees, they probably quote an hourly rate, and it is likely to run into three figures.

Hesitating to go ahead

'But surely they receive commission from the insurance company, or whoever else you do your business with, after you have taken their advice?'

That may be true. You can negotiate with them, about that, before you engage them. You are entitled to know what payment an adviser will receive from an insurance company or other pension provider. It is always wise to find that out, and to learn the *precise basis* on which the adviser will calculate the charges, before you start asking for advice. If the charges are going to be too steep for you, bearing in mind the size of whatever annual investment you have in mind, you should say, 'No, thank you,' and make your escape.

If the kind of fee mentioned is out of proportion to the amount you were contemplating investing, you might be wiser to study one of the magazines that publishes comparative tables of pension providers' results in the past – see Further Reading at the end of this book.

Narrowing the field

If you feel that you are approaching an area you know nothing about, and you want an introduction, you could contact the Money Management National Register of Fee Based Advisers. Useful Addresses at the end of this book tells you how to contact the Register. They will send you a list of several such advisers in your area. They do not charge for the service.

ENSURING THAT YOU AND YOUR PARTNER UNDERSTAND THE ADVICE

You hope that you and your partner will both be benefiting from the advice you receive for many years, so it is important that you both understand that advice. It may greatly affect the incomes and other resources of both of you, in retirement.

TRYING TO GET A SECOND OPINION

The title of this section may seem to imply that you would have difficulty in any attempt to obtain a second opinion. That is not intended. If you were willing to pay for them, you could undoubtedly obtain two, three or as many more opinions as you wished to have.

They might differ so widely that you wondered whether the advisers were dealing with the same set of facts. They might leave you on the horns of a dilemma, uncertain which way to go and wondering whether you had wasted your money, in seeking advice.

Approaching the subject from a different angle

Have you a friend or former colleague who may have some experience of facing your problem? If you have, how about having a chat with him or her about the subject, before you approach a possible adviser? You could regard this as getting a second opinion first – without having to pay for it.

Your objective would be to discuss with this person:

- how he or she had dealt with the problem
- whether a different approach might have been better
- any particular matters one ought to watch out for
- what one needs to say to any adviser one approaches.

Airing the subject, in this way, might put you in a better position to approach an adviser. The more you have talked about your circumstances and the choices that may be open to you, before you approach an adviser, the more effectively you should be able to put your position to him or her and obtain reliable advice.

Meeting an adviser

You will have primed yourself for:

- asking the adviser the right questions

- giving the adviser the right information about your situation unambiguously

- understanding the adviser's suggestions and asking searching questions about any matters that may seem to have been glossed over.

Make sure that you obtain maximum value for the adviser's fee, **including precise recommendations, in writing**.

CHECKLIST

- Know what you want to ask an adviser.

- Choose an adviser:
  - who has preferably been recommended by a reliable person
  - who has recognised qualifications
  - whose basis of fees is justified by your intended outlay on pension
  - who tells you precisely what commission he or she would receive.

- Study the tables of past achievements of approved pension providers in financial journals. They may:
  - help you to form an opinion of any advice you receive
  - encourage you to be your own adviser, if your outlay will be modest.

Glossary

This glossary includes not only expressions that are used in the text of this book but also some that the reader may encounter elsewhere, in connection with pensions.

Actuary. A specialist in the application of mathematics to life assurance and pensions, who is a Fellow of either the Institute of Actuaries or the Faculty of Actuaries.

Added years. An addition to a member's actual years of service, for pension purposes, given because of a transfer value received from the member's previous employer.

Additional voluntary contributions (AVCs). Contributions made voluntarily by a member to boost his other scheme benefits, within Inland Revenue limits.

Administrator. The person or persons resident within the United Kingdom who have the management of the scheme.

Annuity. A contract by which a life office undertakes to make a series of payments depending on the duration of one or more lives.

Appropriate personal pension. An arrangement by a pension provider that enables an employee to contract out of SERPS while not being a member of a contracted out occupational scheme.

Approved scheme. A pension scheme approved by the Inland Revenue as satisfying their requirements.

Beneficiary. A person who is entitled to receive a benefit under a scheme.

Commission. Payment made by a pension provider to an adviser who has introduced a client.

Commutation. Substitution of a single cash payment for an entitlement to payments of pension.

Compulsory purchase annuity. The purchase of an annuity to comply with a requirement that an accumulated fund must be used to provide a pension.

Contributions. Sums paid into a pension fund by the employer or the members, in accordance with the rules of a scheme.

Deferred pensioner. A scheme member who has left the employment but whose benefit entitlement remains a responsibility of the scheme.

Dependant. A person who is financially dependent on another.

Discretionary benefits. Scheme benefits, the payment of which is in some way subject to the discretion of the trustees.

Earnings cap. The maximum net relevant earnings taken into account when allowing tax relief on contributions to a personal pension.

Exempt approved scheme. A retirement benefits scheme established under trust and governed by rules approved by the Inland Revenue.

Final remuneration. An annual rate of pay calculated by reference to a member's earnings, in the period that precedes the ending of his or her employment, in accordance with a formula approved by the Inland Revenue.

Final salary scheme. A scheme that relates the benefits provided for a member in retirement to his or her earnings at, or shortly before, retirement.

Free-standing AVC scheme (FSAVC scheme). A scheme established by an approved pension provider to accept AVCs from members of approved occupational pension schemes.

Incapacity. Physical or mental deterioration that is bad enough to prevent an individual from following his or her normal employment, or that seriously impairs his or her earning capacity.

Independent financial adviser. An adviser who is not tied to any pension provider, but recommends the provider that he or she believes would be best for the client.

Insured scheme. Pension scheme arranged with a life office that provides administration and investment management, and cover for mortality risks.

Life office. A life assurance company, or the life department of a composite insurance company.

Mutual life office. A life office that has no shareholders. It belongs to its with profit policyholders.

Net relevant earnings. An individual's earnings, net of prescribed deductions: the maximum contribution that may be made to a personal pension is a percentage of net relevant earnings.

Normal pension (or retirement) age. The age at which a member of a scheme is expected to retire, in accordance with the rules of the scheme.

Personal pension. A pension bought by an individual's own contributions while self-employed or in non-pensionable employment.

Proprietary life office. A life office that is owned by shareholders.

Protected rights. The part of a fund that is accumulated from rebates of NI contributions in respect of contracting out of pension provision on a money purchase basis.

Purchased life annuity. An annuity paid for by the annuitant from his or her own resources.

Qualifying year. A complete tax year throughout which the full rate of NI contribution was paid.

Relevant benefits. Benefits that may be provided by a retirement benefits scheme.

Retirement annuity contract. The previous version of what is now a personal pension. It was not acceptable for contracting out of SERPS.

Retirement benefits scheme. A scheme for providing relevant benefits for one or more employees.

SERPS. The state earnings-related pension scheme that was set up in 1978 to provide pensions related to earnings between the lower and upper earnings limits.

Small self-administered scheme. A self-administered scheme, usually with not more than 12 members, designed to take advantage of the removal of the ban on controlling directors as members of schemes.

State pension age. The age at which someone who is entitled to receive a state pension may start to draw it.

Transfer value. The cash sum that the trustees of a scheme are willing to pay to extinguish their liability to pay benefits for a member who is joining another scheme.

Trust deed. Document that creates a legal situation relating to the funds of a pension scheme. It appoints trustees to be responsible for ensuring that the funds are dealt with and used in accordance with the rules of the scheme.

Trustee. Person appointed to have the legal ownership of the assets of a trust and the power and duty to oversee their use.

Winding up. The process of realising the assets of a scheme, allocating them to provide immediate or deferred benefits for members and their widows and dependants, and terminating the scheme.

Further Reading

PENSION GUIDES

A Guide to Retirement Pensions, Benefits Agency Leaflet 46.
Good Non-Retirement Guide, Rosemary Brown (Kogan Page, 1998).
Moneywise Guide to Your Pension, Keith Carlton (Readers Digest Assoc, 1998).
Pension Power, Debbie Harrison (John Wiley, 1995).
The Allied Dunbar Pensions Handbook, Anthony Reardon (Pitman, 1997).
Your Rights 1998/9, Age Concern England.

FINANCIAL ADVICE

Be Your Own Financial Adviser, Jonquil Lowe (Consumers Association 1998).
Perfect Personal Finance, Marie Jennings (Arrow 1996).

MONTHLY MAGAZINES

Money Management
Planned Savings

(See also the list of other titles in this series at the front of the book.)

Useful Addresses

REGULATION OF FINANCIAL SERVICES

The Financial Services Authority, Gavrelle House, 2–14 Bunhill Row, London EC1Y 8RA. Tel: general enquiries – charged at local rate – 0845 606 1234. Enquiries relating to specific sectors, referred to in Figure 12, should be made to the following addresses.

Building Societies Commission, Victory House, 30/34 Kingsway, London WC2B 6ES. Tel: (0171) 663 5000.

Registry of Friendly Societies (Address and Tel: as for Building Societies Commission).

Friendly Societies Commission (Address and Tel: as for Building Societies Commission).

Supervision and Surveillance Division of the Bank of England, Threadneedle Street, London EC2R 8AH. Tel: (0171) 601 4878.

Insurance Directorate of the Department of Trade and Industry, 1 Victoria Street, London SW1H 0ET. Tel: (0171) 215 0200.

Investment Management Regulatory Organisation (IMRO), 5th Floor, Lloyds Chambers, Portsoken Street, London E1 8BT. Tel: (0171) 5777.

Personal Investment Authority (PIA), 1 Canada Square, Canary Wharf, London E14 5AZ. Tel: (0171) 538 8860.

Securities and Futures Authority (SFA), Cottons Centre, Cottons Land, London SE1 2QB. Tel: (0171) 378 9000.

ADVISORY BODIES

Insurance Brokers Registration Council, 63 St. Mary Axe, London EC3A 8NB. Tel: (0171) 621 1061. Established under the Insurance Brokers (Registration) Act 1977 to register insurance brokers and regulate their professional standards.

British Insurance & Investment Brokers' Association, BIIBA House, 14 Bevis Marks, London EC3A 7NT. Tel: (0171) 623 9043. Aims to ensure that brokers and their staffs are well trained and kept up-to-date in their knowledge of their subject.

OPAS LTD, 11 Belgrave Road, London SW1V 1RB. Tel: (0171) 233 8080. The Pensions Advisory Service was establised to help people who have a problem that cannot be solved by the people who run their company pension scheme or personal pension plan. Enquirers should give as full information as possible. OPAS does **not** deal with Social Security.

The Pensions Ombudsman, 6th Floor, 11 Belgrave Road, London SW1V 1RB. Tel: (0171) 834 9144. The Ombudsman is an independent and impartial arbitrator who decides complaints and disputes concerning occupational pension schemes. *He should not be approached until OPAS has been contacted.*

UNCLASSIFIED

The Money Management Register of Fee Based Advisers, Gossard House, 7/8 Savile Row, London W1X 1AF. Tel: (0171) 734 8334. Send full address of your home and work (including postcode) for free list of advisers in your area.

U3A National Office, 26 Harrison Street, London WC1 8JG. Tel: (0171) 837 8838. The office will give any applicants the name and details of the person to contact for the nearest branch.

Index

SAVING AND INVESTING
How to achieve financial security and make your money grow

John Whiteley

This book is written by John Whiteley, an experienced practising Chartered Accountant. His work brings him in contact with people from all walks of life. He draws on this experience to bring to light some simple guidelines that will enable you to decide your own financial goals and priorities, make your plans, manage your investments, and monitor the results.

144pp. illus. 1 85703 289 6.

MANAGING YOUR PERSONAL FINANCES
How to achieve financial security and survive the shrinking welfare state

John Claxton

This book, now revised and updated, will help you to prepare a strategy towards creating your own financial independence. Find out in simple language: how to avoid debt, how to prepare for possibly incapacity or redundancy, and how to finance your retirement, including care in old age. Discover how to acquire new financial skills, increase your income, reduce outgoings, and prepare to survive in a more self-reliant world. John Claxton is a Chartered Management Accountant and Chartered Secretary. He teaches personal money management in adult education.

160pp. illus. 1 85703 254 3. 2nd edition.

INVESTING IN STOCKS & SHARES
A step-by-step handbook for the prudent investor

Dr John White

This book has been specially updated to help and guide those with a lump sum or surplus income to invest, and who are considering investing in quoted securities. Dr John White, an Oxford graduate, is himself an experienced investor and advisor to an investment company. 'User-friendly... Contains many practical examples and illustrations of typical share-dealing documents. There are also case studies which give you a feel for your own inclinations about risk versus profit... Demystifies the world of stocks and shares.' *OwnBase.*

224pp illus. 1 85703 369 8. 3rd edition